Don Black is

the world's leading

Boulevard, Tell Me on a

Whistle Down the Wind, B
such as *The Italian Job, The P* carder *strikes Again, True Grit,*
Dances with Wolves and *Out of Africa*. He is the recipient of an
Oscar, two Tonys, a Golden Globe and five Ivor Novello Awards.

Praise for *The Sanest Guy in the Room*

'Among the brilliant stories and wonderful behind-the-scenes glimpses of a life and career in show-business is some great advice, the best of which is don't use fifty words when you can use five. So I won't. Here's what I think of Don's book . . . It's bloody brilliant . . . Read it!'

Michael Ball

'Emotional and poignant'

Jewish Telegraph

'Deeply moving'

Radio Times

'Warm, unpretentious and never lacking in humour'

Mojo

'Breezy and unpretentious, *The Sanest Guy in the Room* is a delightful collection of memories, insider information and after-dinner anecdotes'

The Times

'Somewhere between a memoir and an extended love letter to his late wife, Shirley – who died in 2018, after a marriage that lasted sixty years – it details his remarkable career as a songwriter . . . as down-to-earth and charming as the book's title suggests'

The Guardian

'[Black] sprinkles his memoir with warm reminiscences and self-deprecating anecdotes . . . you'll come away from this entertaining book with a new appreciation for a craft that's too often overlooked'

Mail on Sunday

'One of the joys of Black's memoir is his close-up view of the abnormality of the people he has worked with. He has a sharp eye and turn of phrase . . . Black may well be one of the sanest guys in the room. He's one of the kindest too'

The Herald

The Sanest Guy in the Room

A Life in Lyrics

Don Black

CONSTABLE

CONSTABLE

First published in Great Britain in 2020 by Constable
This paperback edition published in 2021 by Constable

1 3 5 7 9 10 8 6 4 2

A CIP catalogue record for this book
is available from the British Library.

ISBN: 978-1-47213-294-9

Typeset in Minion Pro by SX Composing DTP, Rayleigh, Essex
Printed and bound in Great Britain by Clays Ltd, Elcograf S.p.A.

Papers used by Constable are from well-managed forests
and other responsible sources.

Constable
An imprint of
Little, Brown Book Group
Carmelite House
50 Victoria Embankment
London EC4Y 0DZ

An Hachette UK Company

www.hachette.co.uk
www.littlebrown.co.uk

For Shirley – no one will ever be more missed

STRAIGHT TO THE POINT

If you write to impress it will always be bad, but if you write to express it will be good. **Thornton Wilder**

I have never been a fan of autobiographies. I find all of them way too long, full of boring pages about stuff I'm not at all interested in. I only want to know about the subject, not about the subject's grandparents who may have come from Lithuania, or the subject's aunt who may have been a Windmill girl.

The first thing you learn as a lyric writer is not to waste a syllable, and that you have to eliminate the unnecessary. Lyric writing is all about compression and getting to the nitty-gritty. I guess that's why I find it numbingly tedious when these books veer away from the reason I bought the book in the first place.

So I'm going to have a go at writing my story without the long-winded passages that would start you yawning. I'll try to stick to the important bits to keep your attention. I will write about my times with legendary people like Billy Wilder and Barbra Streisand and Michael Jackson, and the producers and directors I've worked with on five James Bond movies, but I refuse to write chapter after chapter about the long sweeping gravelled paths to their luxurious homes. I want to write about the first time I sat down to write with Andrew Lloyd Webber and not waste a paragraph to ramble on about the warm summer breeze that was blowing in a westerly direction at the time. Who cares?

1

This habit of mine of always cutting to the chase has played havoc with my family. They know when they speak to me they have to edit themselves and get straight to the bottom line. I'll give you an example: when most husbands come home after a day's work they may say gently to their wives, 'Did anyone call while I was out, darling?' When I come home I just yell out, 'Messages?'

How my gorgeous wife Shirley stayed with me for more than sixty years is an unsolvable mystery. Every time she would tell me a story she tried her hardest to shorten it to make sure I was still listening. This book will be as much about Shirley as it will about me. To quote lines from a couple of old songs, once I saw her 'across a crowded room' we were 'as close as pages in a book'.

Apart from those boring, padded passages in autobiographies, I am always sceptical of their veracity. Some publishers are so keen on enhancing the chances of getting a deal with a national paper for the serial rights that books are peppered with sensational anecdotes – it is a legal fact that you can't libel the dead.

I could easily write now that Noël Coward assaulted me when I visited him on the set of *The Italian Job*. I could also speak of a brief but torrid affair I had with Lauren Bacall while she was appearing in a Broadway musical. I could also hint at something going on between me and Ingrid Bergman when I wrote a song for a film called *A Walk in the Spring Rain* in which she starred with Anthony Quinn. None of these things happened, although the Ingrid Bergman fantasy did cross my mind.

This may end up a short book, but hopefully it will end up as one of the few memoirs that you will finish.

CHILDHOOD

Youth is believing that some day you'll dance like
Fred Astaire. **Jacqueline Friedrich** (Journalist)

I had a fantastically happy childhood. We lived in a council flat in Shore Place, Hackney. I know that memories are selective but I can't think of one bad one for the life of me. When I was born I had jaundice and from then on the family called me The Chinaman. Being the youngest of five I was spoiled a lot. My mother hated to wake me up to go to school; she would say 'He's having such a lovely sleep.' My father was an under-presser, which meant he ironed things. My brother Myer, who changed his name to Michael, was something to do with show business – agent, comedian-impressionist, a man about town. My other brother Cyril was a window dresser and also fancied himself as a comedian. My two sisters Nita and Adele were always looking after me. No one has ever had a more supportive family than me. If they read a review saying Don Black's lyrics were awful, they would say 'It could have been worse, they could have said appalling.'

As for me, the only subject I was any good at in school was English. I would have been okay at comedy but they didn't teach that in Cassland Road School in Hackney. Why comedy? Well I was glued to the BBC's light programme in those days and knew most of the routines of Frankie Howerd, Derek Roy, Al Read and the rest. Later on I was fixated on American comics like Woody

Allen, Milton Berle, Alan King and Don Rickles. I was always impressed by the great one-liner funny men. That throwaway type of humour appealed to me. I've also always been impressed by those short, witty, trenchant remarks that say so much with so few words. I'll be quoting some of my favourites throughout this book. I've done this for the whole of my adult life, and looking at them now I think they say a lot about the sort of bloke I am.

When I was about twelve years old my mother had a serious operation. She had a tumour on the brain which thankfully was successfully removed and proved to be benign. All the family were so relieved and we were anxious to show our appreciation to a Mr. Atkinson, the brilliant surgeon who performed the operation. Danny Kaye was appearing at The Palladium then and it was impossible to get tickets. So I wrote to Danny and told him I had to get two tickets for Mr. Atkinson and we didn't care how much we paid. I took the note by hand to the Palladium stage door and a couple of days later we heard from his assistant that he would be happy for us to have two free tickets and he wished my mother a speedy recovery. Since that day Danny Kaye could do no wrong in my eyes.

My closest friend at that time was a boy called Laurence Graff. He lived in Meynell Gardens and we met where all the local Jewish boys went to learn Hebrew and to prepare for their bar mitzvah. This is when a boy of thirteen is supposed to become a man. Our local synagogue was in Ainsworth Road and we both became men at the same time. Laurence was always interested in the jewellery business and it's no surprise to me that he is now regarded as the most successful diamond merchant in the world. In the Sunday Times Rich List his wealth is put at well over three billion pounds! A few years ago we stayed at his sumptuous house in Cap Ferrat. He said to me one day 'Did you ever see *Sixty Minutes*, the programme they did on me in the States?' I said I hadn't and he played the DVD to me and my wife Shirley. At one point the narrator said 'Laurence Graff has worked his way up from London's East End to be worth an estimated two billion dollars.' At that moment his wife Anne Marie entered and when she heard this she said 'This must be an old programme!' Laurence's first job was as an apprentice in Hatton Garden while my first job was as an office boy at the *New Musical Express*. Graff Diamonds has around sixty outlets all over the world and if you call them up and you're put on hold you'll hear Shirley Bassey singing the lyrics I wrote for 'Diamonds Are Forever'.

NME

If your skirt is short enough the party comes to you.
Dorothy Parker

The *New Musical Express* offices were in Denmark Street, which was known as Tin Pan Alley. This small street, which was accurately called two hundred yards of hokum, was populated by music publishers who were selling their songs. This is where I got to meet so many brilliantly talented songwriters. Most days I would be sharing cups of tea with the men who wrote 'My Prayer', 'South of the Border', 'I Saw Mommy Kissing Santa Claus', 'Red Sails in the Sunset', 'Lady of Spain', 'Teddy Bears' Picnic' and dozens more. These were great days – I went to work feeling everything was possible. I was young and as fearless as a knife thrower's assistant. The first megastar I ever met was Nat King Cole. The chief reporter at the paper was Mike Butcher and he said it would be great experience for me if I went along to see how you conduct an interview. Nat wrote the song 'Straighten Up and Fly Right' and Mike asked him why he didn't write more songs. Nat said 'I got lucky with that one but take a song like "I'm gonna sit right down and write myself a letter and make believe it came from you" – who the hell thinks like that?'

Practically all these writers never seemed to age. There was always a twinkle in their eye and a spring in their step. I later learned that this is not the case with all songwriters. Al Dubin

6

('I Only Have Eyes For You' and '42nd Street') was a well-known alcoholic, as was Lorenz Hart. Bob Merrill ('How Much Is That Doggie in the Window' and 'Funny Girl') was a manic depressive who took his own life.

Around that time I met the dynamic Lionel Bart and we stayed friends all through his turbulent life. It was so sad to see him go from wunderkind to spent force. When he died I was asked to write an obituary for a music magazine:

REMEMBERING LIONEL

I loved talking to Lionel. He spoke in a hushed Cockney lilt and used phrases that had more surprises than a magician's sleeve. If he had been more of a public figure he would have been an impressionist's dream. He was flamboyant in a stylish way. Sometimes he arrived dressed as a riverboat gambler or a Mexican peasant complete with sombrero, or in the latest Armani creation. Whatever he wore, as my mother would say, suited him.

His contribution to musical theatre and popular music cannot be exaggerated, and yet, when he became an elder statesman, he held no resentment, no bitterness or envy. He admitted that there were about fifteen years of his life that he couldn't remember – 'Lost somewhere between Vodka and Vine, my love.'

Having lunch with him made you wish you had a tape recorder with you. He would speak of Noël Coward, Judy Garland and Terence Rattigan as 'mates'. Last time we met he spoke of a holiday he had in Miami's famous South Beach, notoriously known as a gay haven. Lionel wasn't impressed 'Too much in yer face. A bit previous'.

He always had many projects simmering. Many were the same old ones he had been dreaming about for years. Musicals of *La Strada*, *Gulliver's Travels* and *The Hunchback of Notre Dame* were three he could never let die away. Anyway, they kept him happy and in contact with directors, producers and other writers. Lionel hated to be alone. He loved collaboration. It seemed that those addictions that lacerated his giant talent had been replaced with a need to be with people, a hunger to belong.

I only saw him angry once. It was a couple of years back when *The Sunday Times* did a survey of people who had an influence on musical theatre. His name was not included and that hurt him. To me it was nothing short of heresy. *Oliver!* alone would put him firmly in that exalted arena alongside Rodgers and Hammerstein, Irving Berlin and the like.

Some years ago at The Vivian Ellis Awards I gave him an introduction that he adored. I subsequently did this many times but never changed the following words:

> It is interesting to note that most of the great legendary composers and lyricists can be identified by their Christian names . . . Jerome, Oscar, Cole, Lorenz, Ira . . . well we have one here tonight and all I have to say is Ladies and Gentlemen . . . Lionel.

Everyone who met him will be richer for it. Someone like him only happens once. When someone who works in the same factory as you, so to speak, dies, you are left with a feeling of enormous sadness coupled with the priceless elation that comes from treasured memories. Or as Lionel would have put it – 'it sort of does yer head in'.

SHIRLEY

Love makes everything bearable. **Carl Sagan**

Sometimes a single moment changes all the ones that follow. That moment for me was when I met a seventeen-year-old girl called Shirley Berg. It was at a social club called The Harmony Club in Clapton. I was sixteen and we were married for almost sixty gloriously happy years. I've joked in the past that I fell in love with her when I went to her parents' flat for dinner and noticed that they had matching plates. That isn't true; what attracted me to her – apart from her being beautiful – was that she read books and she cried when she heard touching songs. In sixty-odd years I never knew her to be in a bad mood unless I put her in one. People ask me if I've ever written a song especially for her and my answer is, 'Yes, all of them.' She has been and will always be my secret weapon. I remember her saying to me a few days after we met that she was going to stay in and wash her hair that night but decided to go to the club. My life would have been very different if she had stayed in. Throughout our married life if we had a little tiff she would say, 'I knew I should have stayed in and washed my hair!'

I began writing this book around January 2018. Shirley read the first half a dozen pages and said she thought it was fresh and different and that I should carry on with it. On 7 March 2018 my precious Shirley's golden heart stopped beating. She picked up a fungal infection on holiday in Miami, or on the plane home. It doesn't really matter where or when. It affected her breathing and after spending almost a month in the Chelsea and Westminster hospital, where they tried everything, she contracted sepsis and bravely lost her battle.

She has left an overwhelming void in all our lives that Steinbeck, Hemingway and Tolstoy would find impossible to describe. I will finish this book, not only for Shirley, but selfishly for me. Every word brings her closer. You may now find that my sentences will get longer. Soon after she left us I had an emotional call from Andrew Lloyd Webber who said that Shirley's passing had an enormous impact on him and he had written a melody to celebrate 'a remarkable lady'. It was a personal present for me and my family. The tune was magnificent and it took me about twenty minutes to write the words.

> Shirley never left me
> Even for one day
> She would never let go
> No that was not her way
>
> Shirley's all around me
> We're not far apart
> How could I feel alone
> While she is in my heart
>
> True love goes on
> Year to endless year
> Shirley never left me
> Shirley is right here

About eighteen months later I had a call from a talented young songwriter called Jack McManus. He is married to singer Martine McCutcheon. He was working with Michael Ball and Michael told him to send me a tune that he loved. As soon as I heard what Jack sent through I thought it was the perfect melody to write about loss and how I was dealing with it. It has recently been recorded by Michael Ball and Alfie Boe:

'I will always believe'

I will always believe
You're still here with me
And the memory of you
Outshines every day
I'll always believe you hear me when I pray
You're still here
Here to stay

You play a part
In everything I try to do
Nothing has changed
I'm still relying on you now
The same way as I've always done
Two people who became one
And stayed as one

I will always believe
I'm never alone
Every road that I walk
I'm not on my own

11

I'll always believe you
Are keeping me strong
As you did all along

Some days when I feel I've lost my way
I get back on my feet
By asking what would you do?
What would you say?

I will always believe
You're still here with me
And the memory of you
Outshines every day
I'll always believe you hear me when I pray
You're still here
Here to stay

I will always believe
I'm never alone
Every road that I walk
I'm not on my own
I'll always believe you are keeping me strong
As you did all along

I mentioned my loss on my radio show and was inundated with letters and emails from listeners expressing their sadness. My friends all seemed to offer the same advice: work, work, work. I have taken their advice and have said yes to practically any work I've been offered. This memoir is a godsend, as is my radio show.

I have never cooked a thing in my life and Shirley dealt with all the boring stuff like car insurance and VAT and plumbers and the garden. I have no idea how I will get my head around all this. My main concern is keeping myself together for my sons, Grant and Clive. I know I have to be strong. They have only known happiness and their perfect world, like mine, has been blown apart.

I don't think I will ever get over the absence of the familiar.

I think it was Judi Dench who said when she lost her husband 'You will find lots of people to do lots of things with, but no one to do nothing with.'

| SHORTHAND

I left the NME after five years and from my time there one memory is as vivid now as it was then. I started off at the NME as an office boy, then moved up into the circulation department and then advertising. What I really wanted was to become a member of the editorial staff. Shirley was a terrific shorthand typist and said that she would teach me shorthand and it would prove to be very valuable if I was going to be a reporter. She spent ages trying to teach me this curious skill. I eventually got a bit of a grasp of it. Everyone on the paper knew I was learning shorthand and one night the owner of the paper, a delightful starstruck man called Maurice Kinn, came up to me in a sweaty panic. He was about to receive a call from Los Angeles with news of stars who were coming over to London. All the secretaries had gone home and he asked me if I could take the information down in short-hand. It was obviously a very important long-distance call and Mr Kinn thanked me profusely before it came in and he shouted out what he wanted me to take down. It went something like this. 'Frankie Laine for two weeks at the Palladium April 3rd, Johnny Ray at The Talk of The Town May 9th for three weeks, Danny Kaye for a month at the Palladium July 7th'. This went on for quite a bit and I was scribbling furiously. When I finished Mr Kinn was over the moon and never stopped thanking me. He said, 'Type it all up and you can have the day off tomorrow.' I then went into Peter Charlesworth's office who, I later found out, was the only news editor in the world who couldn't spell 'and'. I looked at my shorthand and was shocked to see that I couldn't decipher most of what I had written. I told Peter, who uttered a sentence that has stayed with me and my family for more than sixty years. He said, 'You have no option but to go in and say, "Mr Kinn, I have over-reached myself."' All I could think to do was to phone Shirley and ask her to come and see if she could read it. She rushed to my office and looked and tried her hardest to figure out what I'd done but she couldn't. I had no other option but to say that sentence, 'Mr. Kinn, I have overreached myself.' It was greeted with a forced rictus grin followed by a look of deep melancholia. He couldn't find words so he just ushered me out with a wave of his sweaty hand. I still remember quite a bit of shorthand and if you asked me to write down 'The cow jumped over the moon' I'm sure I could do it faster than you.

I then moved across the street to the David Toff Music Publishing Company. It was my job to plug the songs they published and we had a couple of big hits during my time there – 'Don't Laugh at Me' by Norman Wisdom and 'Que Sera Sera' by Doris Day. I mingled with songwriters even more then – Barry Mason ('Delilah'), Les Reed ('It's Not Unusual'), Mitch Murray ('How Do You Do It?'). I still meet some of those writers but these days it's usually in Harley Street rather than Denmark Street.

MATT MONRO AND STAND-UP COMEDY

The audience was with me all the way, I managed to shake them at the station. **Bob Hope**

M y best friend from the moment we met in the fifties to the day he died in 1985 was Matt Monro. When I first knew him he had just given up his day job as a bus driver to try and make a living as a singer. In those days singers would get paid for demonstrating new songs for music publishers. I was in a position to hire him from time to time and pay him the princely sum of five pounds per song. It may not sound a lot but Matt was living from fiver to fiver back then.

I was getting a bit fed up plugging songs and was toying with the idea of becoming a stand-up comedian. I did this professionally for a couple of years and played some of the most famous music halls in the country: The Metropolitan, Edgware Road; Collins Music Hall; Woolwich Empire and quite a few more. Coincidentally they all closed down after I played them! I blame myself entirely for the death of Variety. I tell people that I wrote my first song while waiting for a laugh in Darlington. I like to think that I was ahead of my time but the truth is I looked very young and I was doing material that was best suited to a middle-aged man. No surprise really because I stole my material from middle-aged American comedians.

One of my most forgettable gigs was when I played The Panama Club in Windmill Street. I was doing five shows a day

16

and I came on in between the strippers. The audience was made up of priapic young men and fantasising old ones. Comedy was the last thing on their minds. Matt used to come in during my 'act' and talk to me from the stalls! He would say 'Hello son, when you've finished here why don't we go for a drink at the White Lion?' I would then have a chat with him from the stage and when he left I carried on with the 'jokes'. Strangely enough the audience didn't even notice Matt's interruptions as they had other things on their minds.

I must say that throughout my career as a comedian my loyal family went to every show and thought I was fabulous.

I went back to Denmark Street and plugged more songs for a while, and then a role reversal took place. Matt was making a bit of a name for himself and he remembered those fivers I lavished on him. He asked me to be his manager, which is something I did for more than twenty years. Sometimes, if you're lucky, you meet someone who makes you see life differently. Matt did that to me. He became a huge international star, winning all kinds of awards and gold records. He was admired by Frank Sinatra and Tony Bennett and songwriters Johnny Mercer and Hoagy Carmichael. He was without doubt the best singer ever to come out of this country. And yet he never changed one iota from the day I met him in Denmark Street. He was the most down-to-earth star you could ever wish to meet; just as happy chatting to the postman as he was having a drink with Shirley Bassey. I went all around the world with Matt and never really saw any of it. He was happier having a game of cards in a hotel than walking along Ipanema beach or Fifth Avenue. Something that happened once summed up Matt brilliantly. I have to explain first that the most popular television show at the time was *Crown Court*. It was on every afternoon and it was a gripping court-case drama. I had been trying for ages to set up a meeting for Matt with the great impresario Bernard Delfont. I called him and I couldn't wait to blurt out the exciting news that Mr Delfont had agreed to a meeting next Friday. Matt's instant reaction was 'Oh for Christ's sake, Don, not Friday, that's the day they give the verdict!'

It was Matt who encouraged me to write lyrics. He fell in love with an Austrian melody by Udo Jürgens called 'Warum, nur Warum'. I remember him saying to me, 'You're always on about lyrics – if Lionel Bart can do it so can you.' I called the song 'Walk Away' and it went to number two in the hit parade. I then went on to write about thirty songs for Matt including my Oscar-winning one 'Born Free'. But my success as a writer meant I had less time for Matt. This was a difficult time for me because I loved Matt and we were a great team together. I began writing with Henry Mancini, Elmer Bernstein, Quincy Jones, Marvin Hamlisch, and I also wrote musicals with John Barry and Broadway's Jule Styne and Andrew Lloyd Webber. Many times I felt I should be with Matt when he was appearing in nightclubs in Manchester and Newcastle but I had offers to work with great Hollywood composers and I was always torn between my burgeoning career and Matt's deeply felt friendship. Eventually we agreed that someone else should take over his management and we stayed close until the end. Not a day goes by when I don't think about this ordinary man with an extraordinary talent. Matt was wonderful company; always ready with a hearty laugh and I still get goose bumps when I hear him sing. I play a Matt Monro record on my radio show every week. The Beatles producer George Martin, who also produced Matt, said: 'Matt had one of the best pop voices I've ever heard. He was a little guy, but he could produce the most wonderful note and hang onto it for ages. The fact that he smoked sixty to eighty cigarettes a day and drank about a bottle of brandy a night made no difference. He was able to produce this glorious sound.'

I still remember Matt's phone numbers in Ewell and Ealing. Unfortunately he was a heavy drinker and it was heartbreaking to see his health diminish over the years. When he was dying he was still smiling and that really threw me. He wasn't a religious man but he did have faith and that faith kept his spirits up. He said to me at the end 'I would rather leave the world at fifty-four than live like Johnny Mathis drinking only milk all the fucking time.'

I have so many memories of Matt Monro's last days. I remember him receiving a telegram that made him so happy, it read: Dear Matt, Sorry to hear you've been taken ill and hope you'll soon be on the mend and up and about. I send you love and prayers. Your fellow boy singer, Frank Sinatra.

Matt was very brave. I went to visit him at Addenbrooke's Hospital in Cambridge as he was about to go undergo a liver transplant operation. The nurse came in to give him his pre-med pill and I said, 'I'll see you later.' He said, 'Hang about son, these pills take ages to work.' So I stayed around his bed with Shirley and a man called John Ashby, who took over from me as Matt's manager.

The three of us then went over the road to have lunch at the University Arms Hotel. They had records playing and one of the songs that came on brought a shiver down our spines, it was Matt singing, 'Softly As I Leave You'. The operation was aborted as Matt's cancer had spread everywhere. But how apt and prophetic was that choice of song in the University Arms Hotel.

THE SANEST GUY IN THE ROOM

'Walk Away'

Walk away, please go
Before you throw your life away
A life that I
Could share for just a day

We should have met
some years ago
For your sake I say
Walk away, just go

Walk away and live
A life that's full with no regret
Don't look back at me
Just try to forget

Why build a dream
That cannot come true?

So be strong, reach the stars now
Walk away, walk on

If I heard your voice
I'd beg you to stay
So don't say a word
Just run, run away

Goodbye my love,
My tears will fall now that you're gone
I can't help but cry
But I must go on

I'm sad that I

After searching so long

Knew I loved you, but told you

Walk away, walk on

When I was managing Matt Monro in the Sixties and Seventies he played a lot of those Northern clubs. They were amazing places and had the biggest stars; people like Shirley Bassey and Louis Armstrong . . . really big performers. However, some of the people who ran these clubs were totally baffled as to how to handle the stars. I remember booking Matt into the Dolce Vita in Newcastle. I called the manager one day and explained that I was Matt's manager and I was just checking that the piano was in good shape. He said, 'No problem, we've just had it painted!'

A CHIP OFF THE OLD BLOCK

Shirley had the biggest heart and the smallest handwriting. In order to read her notes, I often used to remove my glasses and put them an inch from my eyes. I have called her practical and level-headed but that doesn't mean boring. She was a fabulous dancer and also very funny. In bed one night when it was taking me a while to get excited she said, 'What's the matter, can't you think of anyone?' I also remember having dinner with her in New York with the misnamed Joe Little (who was overweight) and his wife Inga. Joe was Matt's American agent. He said to me, 'Your wife is so wonderful.' I replied, 'Yes, she is, but she's lousy in bed.' And Shirley said quickly, 'He gives me nothing to work with.'

Travelling the world with Matt meant that Shirley did the heavy lifting when it came to bringing up the boys. In those days you had to book international calls and Shirley always made sure the boys were around for my calls. If they were after bedtime she let them stay up for them. In a way this made them happy I was abroad a lot! She used to end every call the same way, 'I love you but this call must be costing a fortune.'

Shirley's father, Jack, was a tough and fearless man raised in the East End. It was the time of Mosley's anti-Semitic movement and Jack would always carry a hammer in his pocket. He was not a religious Jew but he was a proud one. When he became a taxi driver he always had a hammer in his cab. He was extremely protective of his wife and daughters. There's no doubt that Shirley had a streak in her that she inherited from her father.

One day when the four of us were sitting down to dinner in our home in Mill Hill Shirley said to us, 'Don't be surprised if the police come round tonight.' This was probably the most un-Shirley sentence we'd ever heard from her. She explained that she had been in a traffic jam in Edgware when this woman kept hooting her. She couldn't move because there were cars in front of her. This didn't stop the woman hooting and Shirley was getting more riled. Eventually Shirley got out of the car and walked back to the woman who was pointing at Shirley and obviously swearing in a different language. Shirley grabbed her by the hair and the woman's wig came off. She was as bald as a snooker ball and Shirley threw the wig into the gutter. The woman screamed 'Mein Gott, mein Gott!' as Shirley drove off.

Another time Shirley showed this no-nonsense side of her nature was when she received a call from a teacher at Clive's school in Harrow. His name was Nigel Bennett. He said that Clive had been naughty and would she come and pick him up right away. When she got there she learned that six pupils were going to get the cane. Five of them received this punishment but when it came to Clive's turn he refused to put his hand out. Mr Bennett threatened to call his mother and Clive said, 'Go ahead.'

Shirley arrived and when she was told the story, with one hand she swept all the books off Mr Bennett's desk. This six-foot teacher seemed to shrivel and neither Shirley nor Clive went to the school again.

When Clive left school and wanted to get into the music business I called my friend Derek Block who was a big-time agent and concert promoter. Clive went to see him and when he came home he said to Shirley that he thought it went very well. Shirley said 'Forget it, he called before and said that he might find a place for you in his T-shirt merchandising department. I said to him "If I wanted my Clivey selling schmutter he'd be working for his fucking uncle in Islington market." I then hung up on him.'

JOHN BARRY

I first met John Barry in Denmark Street in the early sixties. We would have long conversations about songs, and I remember him telling me how much he liked the melody of 'Cocktails for Two' but how upset he was that the Spike Jones novelty version of the song took all the beauty out of the tune. I would talk to him about the brilliant lyrics of Larry Hart and in particular the song 'Manhattan'. Time passed and eventually I wrote 'Walk Away'. John Barry loved the song, which was about an older man who was in love with a younger girl – something John could relate to! In those days John was the coolest man on the planet. He drove a white Maserati, he wore handmade suits, he had a fabulous bachelor apartment overlooking the Thames. He was handsome, successful and famous – I don't know what those beautiful women saw in him. One miraculous day John asked me if I'd like to have a go at *Thunderball*, the new James Bond film. That was a life-changing moment for me.

Since then I must have written over a hundred songs with John and, I think it's fair to say, I was his only true friend. He was a loner and an introvert and hated being with people he considered phoney or artificial. He drank too much and that's when his Yorkshire bluntness came bursting through. One night at a party in Hollywood, John Phillips of The Mamas and Papas was talking about John's favourite composer, Gustav Mahler, and John thought he was talking rubbish and told him so. John Phillips said, 'Let's settle this outside' and John B, who was painfully thin, was anxious to fight with the six-foot-five, gym-fit singer. It took me and Hank Mancini, Burt Bacharach and Quincy Jones to stop the potential bloodbath. When Michael Caine presented John with an award some years ago he said, 'This is the first time I can remember an award being heavier than the recipient!'

John was never a big eater; in fact, compared to him Gandhi was a glutton. In fifty years of lunches with John I don't remember a single time when the waiter hasn't whispered, 'Is everything all right, Mr. Barry?'

Only the best was good enough for John. It had to be Dom Pérignon Champagne, it had to be Stolichnaya vodka, it had to be Puligny-Montrachet wine, it had to be Delamain brandy . . . and then we'd have lunch.

John lived in Oyster Bay, New York, and he used to swim in his pool every morning and always to Mahler's 5th Symphony – he was obviously a very slow swimmer.

John had quite a few celebrity neighbours including Billy Joel and Jimmy Webb, and living next door were members of the Estée Lauder family. One day his doorbell rang and his beautiful wife Laurie shouted down from her bedroom for me to answer it. I couldn't believe my eyes, it was none other than Rupert Murdoch! He had a towel and swimming trunks under his arm and wanted to use John's pool as his was being renovated. After his swim I had a very long chat with him; he was fascinated that I used to work for the *New Musical Express*. He was absolutely besotted by newspapers and told me that although he owned Fox

Pictures he found it very hard to get excited by films. It was a moment to remember because he seemed so normal, he could have been a fellow bus driver at Matt Monro's depot.

Writing songs with John was an absolute joy and really very easy; he liked uncomplicated, honest lyrics – nothing fancy or clever. Our collaboration was more like a marriage, and like a wonderful marriage it was too short.

He loved a laugh and his favourite comics were Tommy Cooper and W. C. Fields. He was a great audience; I remember telling him a joke in Wiltons, a restaurant he loved in Jermyn Street, and he was hysterical. All I said was 'What's the difference between a Jewish mother and a rottweiler?' He said 'What?' and I said, 'Eventually a rottweiler lets go!' He almost choked on the one chip he did eat.

What really amazed me about John was just how America never changed him one little bit. He lived there for about forty years but he remained a Yorkshireman through and through. Not once did I ever hear him say anything remotely American like 'go figure' or 'I don't have any issues with that', he never used words like 'awesome' or 'closure'. I always felt John put the York in New York.

He was a very private man, not the easiest to get to know, but if you knew him, really knew him, you loved him.

Unfortunately for John and for me and for all of us outside of the Bond world – you only live once.

THE BERGS

Behind every successful songwriter there's an astonished
mother-in-law. **Don Black**

For years I used to get a late-night taxi from Shirley's flat in
Clapton to my flat in Hackney. I could ill afford that five-
shilling taxi ride although it was worth it. It was only after about
three years when I was looking for a taxi home that I saw a bus
coming that went to the top of my street!

Shirley's parents were great characters. They were Jack and Ada
Berg, though she preferred to be called Adele. She was a highly
strung woman, very nervy and full of life. She and her devoted
husband Jack were madly in love for some seventy years. Jack was
a cab driver, and like most cab drivers he had strong views, he
would say stuff like 'There's more crooks in Parliament than there
are in Pentonville.' He also had some very strange sayings that he
learned as a boy. They didn't make any sense at all but he never
stopped laughing at them. Here are a few: 'Everything in his
favour's against him' and 'I know him well, we went to separate
schools together.' 'He was a short feller with long legs.' He didn't
like many people, he thought most were 'potses' or 'tuppeny
ha'ppeny big shots'.

Jack could talk for hours about Churchill, politics, boxing, and
the Chinese. This was the complete opposite of Ada who wasn't at
all interested in what was going on in the world. Whenever she

was asked about something topical she would listen to the question, think for a minute and then say a phrase that has stayed with us all – 'Bother my head'. Jack loved coming to our home and sitting in front of my computer while he watched Bobby Darin sing 'Mack the Knife' or Dorothy Squires sing 'My Way'. I could understand Dorothy Squires but I'm still not sure about 'My Way'.

Ada's life was cursed with bad health. So much so that it became a joke. During her last few years she had asthma, angina, anaemia – and that's only the As! She was a born complainer and not the easiest of patients. I once told her that she was responsible for the premature deaths of fourteen hairdressers, eight carers and nine nurses. Sadly she suffered greatly at the end, having to endure dozens of blood transfusions and unpleasant hospital procedures and relying on oxygen, nebulisers and steroids. This was far different to the woman I knew when I met her. A glamorous lady, full of life, who loved a laugh, a game of kalooki and a jive on the dance floor to Tom Jones singing 'Sex Bomb'.

Shirley's sister Rozlyn was always beautiful and, although now in her eighties, still has a beguiling look. She was known in the family as the wayward one who has never made a cup of tea. She's familiar with the phrase 'Hard work won't kill you' but she has never wanted to take a chance. She had a rocky marriage that just sort of fizzled out. She was, and still is, addicted to smoking. She's had all the warnings but they have no effect on her continued inhaling. Shirley used to speak with her on the phone every day and now whenever we talk on the phone about what great memories we have it always ends with her fighting back the tears.

▌ TO SIR WITH LOVE

'To Sir, With Love' was one of the few lyrics that I wrote before the melody was written. The director, James Clavell, said that the lyric is the most important part because it has to sum up all the deep emotional feelings of the movie. Whenever I'm asked to write a song for a film I like the producer, director or writer to tell me what it's all about in a sentence or two. You may think that I have to read the script or see the film ten times before I put pen to paper, but James said to me, 'It's about a black teacher (Sidney Poitier) who gets a job in London's east end and the kids give him hell. By the end of the film they come to love him.' The words came easily to me because the brief was so specific:

> Those schoolgirl days,
> Of telling tales and biting nails are gone,
> But in my mind,
> I know they will still live on and on.
> But how do you thank someone,
> Who has taken you from crayons to perfume?
> It isn't easy but I'll try.
>
> If you wanted the sky,
> I would write across the sky,
> In letters that would soar a thousand feet high.

'To sir, with love.'

The time has come,
For closing books and long last looks must end.
And as I leave,
I know that I am leaving my best friend.

A friend who taught me right from wrong,
And weak from strong – that's a lot to learn,
What can I give you in return?
If you wanted the moon,
I would try to make a start,
But I would rather you let me give my heart,
To sir, with love.

James Clavell loved the lyric, so now we had to find a tune to go with it. As Lulu was in the film and was going to sing the song we left the choice to her. About a dozen writers had a go at coming up with the melody and she went for the one written by a young Canadian boy called Mark London. She made the right choice because her record of 'To Sir, With Love' went to number one in America and stayed there for five weeks!

You never know when you write a song if it will be a hit or not, but you do know if it's got something special about it; that indefinable and elusive bit of magic. The lyrical thrust of 'To Sir, With Love' has a universal appeal as everyone has either been to or is at school, and we all look back on those days at some point in our lives. I've always tried to find a universal thought in a song because a truly great song isn't for just one person, it's for everyone. If a listener can recognise themselves in a song then you've done something right.

AMERICA

Hollywood is the only place in the world where you can die of encouragement. **Pauline Kael**

I've always been in love with America. It's an easy thing to do when you're brought up in a council flat in Hackney and on the radio you hear songs with magical titles like 'Moonlight in Vermont', 'Stars Fell on Alabama' or 'Give My Regards to Broadway'. In the local Regal cinema, which was just a nondescript walk away from where we lived, you could watch Fred Astaire and Ginger Rogers dancing on white shiny pianos and Gene Kelly *Singin' in the Rain* and Donald O'Connor dancing up walls. American stars seemed to have names that were a million miles from the British stars. We had John Mills and Richard Todd, they had Mitzi Gaynor, Rhonda Fleming, Cyd Charisse and Rory Calhoun.

On other days in the Regal I would be mesmerised by James Cagney and Edward G. Robinson running up and down rickety New York fire escapes trying to outsmart the local cop or vicar, usually played by Pat O' Brien.

When I finally made my first trip to New York with Matt Monro I felt as if I knew those numbered streets and those neon-lit diners. We ate at those delicatessens where huge sandwiches are served by world-weary waiters.

One night I went to the famous Carnegie Jewish deli on 7th Avenue and I said to the lugubrious-looking waiter 'Why do you always give me a lousy table when I come here?' He shouted loudly to a waitress, 'Hey Stella, give this guy a sea view!'

I would pop into P. J. Clarke's bar on 55th Street hoping to bump into Johnny Mercer. He was known to frequent this bar and is said to have written 'One for My Baby' on a napkin there at 'quarter to three' in the morning. The bartender at that time was Tommy Boyce. Johnny apologised to him when he didn't use his name – 'Nothing rhymes with Tom' he said, settling for 'Set 'em up Joe'.

I became a member of the famous Friars Club which was always full of comedians. I got friendly with the man known as 'The king of the one-liners' – Henny Youngman. He couldn't stop using them. When I met him his first words to me were, 'Keep your hair like that, you'll get a lot of laughs'. He introduced me to another comedian and said, 'He needs no introduction, what he needs is an act.' He went on like this all day and I used to walk him home after lunch. Cab drivers would shout his name when they saw him. On one of these walks I had a laughing attack – he said to me 'I read that your friend Lloyd Webber is a billionaire, can that be true?' I said, yes, probably, and he said 'See, if you don't smoke.'

All my New York experiences paid off when I wrote *Tell Me on a Sunday* with Andrew, which is full of the Manhattan observations of a thirty-something British girl from Muswell Hill.

My first trip to Los Angeles was equally overwhelming. The names of the streets are so inviting; Coldwater Canyon, Sunset Boulevard, Rodeo Drive all so much more beguiling than Croydon, Bermondsey or Stepney. The people we met were so energetic and optimistic and it took a while to adjust to their constant bright view of life. I have a theory that it's impossible to have a bad meeting in Los Angeles. No one likes to be the bearer of bad news.

When we all moved to Los Angeles in the seventies I was looking for a house to rent. Now estate agents, or realtors, as they're called over there, have a fantastic thing going for them. They entice you by telling you who lives near you. If you're not too sure if it's the house you're looking for they will say, 'Kirk Douglas lives down the road' or, 'this was Dean Martin's favourite street'. If you're a bit starstruck, and who isn't, it's impossible not to be influenced by this.

The same thing happened to me when I checked into The Algonquin Hotel in New York. I was so disappointed with my room I immediately called down to reception and said, 'This is the smallest, darkest room I've ever been in.' The receptionist replied, 'That's strange, it was Humphrey Bogart's favourite.' I hate to admit it but I then said, 'Don't worry about it, it'll be fine.'

Speaking of shallowness, I remember checking out of the Regency Hotel in New York at 6 a.m. to catch a flight to London. Someone was checking in. We looked at each other and he said, 'You look familiar.' I replied, 'I'll give you a clue, you're my American agent.'

Peter Stone was a famous screenwriter who also wrote the books to two successful musicals – 1776 and Titanic. He thought this was the best Hollywood story he'd ever heard:

A struggling writer, having been told by his agent Mort that Steven Spielberg loved his new novel and was going to turn it into a major movie, buys a new house in Beverly Hills, gets himself a Ferrari and sets his kids up in an expensive school. Barely able to control his excitement, he goes to see Mort, who has an office at Universal Studios. 'Isn't it great?!' he says, 'My whole life is about to change. I tell you, Mort, this is the best thing that's ever happened to me. Thank you so much, Mort.' 'Hang on a minute,' says Mort, 'There's something I've got to tell you. Spielberg decided to pass on your book. He's not going to make the movie. I'm awfully sorry.' Stunned silence. 'Are you telling me it's not going to happen?' says the dumbfounded writer. 'That's what I'm telling you,' says Morty with a shrug. 'It's not going to happen. That's show business, kid.'

'But what about the house I've just bought, and the car, and the school fees? Morty, tell me you're joking.' 'Sorry kid, but Spielberg's passed.'

'The motherfucker!' says the writer. 'He can't do this to me. I'll show the bastard what's what!' And with that he pulls a revolver from his inside jacket pocket. 'What are you doing with that revolver?' says Morty. 'I know Spielberg has an office on the lot. I'll show him he can't treat people this way,' says the writer, and rushes out into the corridor, whereupon Morty quickly gets on the telephone and calls up Spielberg. 'Steven,' he says, 'remember that book you liked then passed on? Well, listen, the writer is so mad at you, he's on his way to your office now with a revolver and he's going to kill you. But that's not why I called.'

I went to Los Angeles, Las Vegas and New York many times as Matt's manager, and although it was thrilling to attend opening nights when people like Jack Benny and Liberace were in the audience, and Tony Bennett and Sammy Davis Jr and Bobby Darin were regular visitors to his shows, for me, personally, it got even better once I won an Oscar in 1966. I was the first British songwriter to win an Oscar and they tell me I was the youngest. I was twenty-seven.

As a result of winning I made a lot of new friends – my kind of friends, talented songwriters and composers: Norman Gimbel ('The Girl from Ipanema'), Arthur Hamilton ('Cry Me a River'), Paul Francis Webster ('Love Is a Many-Splendored Thing'), Sammy Cahn ('Call Me Irresponsible') and many others. I started writing with Henry Mancini, Dave Grusin, Lalo Schifrin and Elmer Bernstein. In between all this heady stuff I was managing Matt Monro, whose career was beginning to soar. So one day I'm with him in Newcastle while he was appearing at La Dolce Vita nightclub and at the same time I'm writing lyrics for a bunch of obscure movies.

I needed an office and a secretary to help me with all this activity, and I was approached by the bandleader and agent Vic Lewis to join him. This was a very exciting period in my life because Vic's little company was bought out by Brian Epstein's company NEMS. My office was next to Brian's and he eventually did a deal with GAC, which was a powerful American agency that represented everyone from Nat King Cole to Groucho Marx. This is where I met so many glittering stars. There was a time when Vic and myself were inseparable, a sort of Jewish Ant and Dec. I will never forget those marvellous meals with the likes of Nelson Riddle, Johnny Mathis, Mel Tormé, Andy Williams, etc.

Vic was one of the world's great hypochondriacs! However, his ailments were most peculiar. He would arrive at the office and say things like, 'I'm not myself today, my hair hurts,' or, 'My tongue feels cold.' He was a passionate stamp collector and wherever we went in the world the first thing he would do would be to buy a sheet of local stamps. We were on our way to Manila with the Everly Brothers and we made a stop in Saigon at the height of the Vietnam war. As soon as we got off the plane we could hear gunfire and we watched the terrified looks on the soldiers' faces. This didn't stop Vic rushing up to the high-ranking official on duty and saying, 'Excuse me, but I save stamps.' The man looked down on Vic said, 'No shit,' and walked away.

One memorable day two young songwriters came to see me called Elton John and Bernie Taupin. They were unhappy with their then manager, Dick James. They asked me if I was interested in managing them. I said to them I'm much too busy and Matt takes up so much of my time. On my radio show recently I told this story and added the line, 'Can you imagine how much bigger they would have been if I took them on!'

BEING A SONGWRITER

Songwriters are the most intuitive people in the world. None of them can explain where the hell their stuff comes from and they're all a little nuts! **Abe Burrows** – Book writer of the musical *Guys and Dolls*

My closest collaborator throughout all of this was still John Barry.

It was easy writing with John – he would hand me a melody and I would go home and put words to it. Although I've often written words first and handed them to a composer, I much prefer it the other way around. If you write the words first there is a tendency to ramble, but if you only have a limited number of notes they provide you with a rigid framework and that enables you to be concise.

Oscar Hammerstein said when he started writing lyrics he was a bit sloppy and lazy until he spoke to the composer Sigmund Romberg who told him that bad work will come back and haunt you. He came up with a wonderful analogy. He said when the Statue of Liberty was erected in the New York Harbour in 1886 no one could have known that one day many years later helicopters would fly over her and see the back of her head. The back of her head that was never seen is as immaculately and painstakingly made as the rest of her. Oscar said from then on he took a little extra time with every word.

When I speak to students they always hope I'll explain how I write lyrics, but the truth is I don't know, it's sort of indefinable. I do tell them to listen to the words of Ira Gershwin, Larry Hart, Oscar Hammerstein, Stephen Sondheim and about a dozen other great wordsmiths. When songwriter Paul Williams (*Bugsy Malone*) was asked where his inspiration comes from he said that he has invisible allies somewhere in his head. It's a clever answer, because, well, at least it is an answer.

Irving Berlin said that he didn't believe in inspiration and that great songs came from hard work. He said that he used to come home from his office in the evening, have dinner and then write, sometimes till 4 or 5 in the morning. He said, and I love this quote, 'talent is only the starting point'.

One of life's greatest pleasures to me is listening to a beautifully crafted song. I can't exaggerate the sheer emotional joy I get from listening to the masters of the Great American Songbook. This is something I've been doing all my life so I know how good a song can be. But if any lyric writers are reading this I'd like to tell them that anyone can write a mediocre lyric. It takes a tremendous amount of hard work to write a great one. You also have to love words with an unrivalled passion. So if you can listen to Oscar Hammerstein and not admire his folksy genius, if you can listen to Stephen Sondheim and not marvel at his graceful solutions, if you can listen to Mercer, Lerner and Hart and not be bowled over by their concise eloquence, and if you can listen to the score of Gershwin's *Porgy and Bess* without getting goose bumps, then forget about writing lyrics, you're not cut out for it.

If one could look into the mind and body of a songwriter when he is in the throes of discovering a fresh chord sequence or an original lyric idea, I think we would find the same characteristics and functions as that of a dog who senses an earthquake before any human. Although there may not be any outside evidence of this elation, inside, bells and Roman candles are going off in all directions.

This almost spiritual feeling is at the very heart and soul of the songwriter. And even though the completed song might end up in a drawer or in Simon Cowell's oversized waste-paper basket, it doesn't stop the emotional surge that comes with fulfilling that magical three-minute dream.

Having said all this, one should not take song writing too seriously. You can spend a lifetime perfecting the craft only to be brought down with a dissonant bang. This was brought home to me with devastating clarity some time ago when I was listening to one of those radio quiz shows. The question was 'Who was the last woman to be hanged in Great Britain?' – without hesitation the answer came back confidently 'Vivian Ellis.' Vivian was the man whose hits included 'Spread a Little Happiness', and is not to be confused with the notorious Ruth Ellis.

> Yip Harburg wrote the lyrics to *The Wizard of Oz*. He also wrote the lyrics to 'April in Paris'. He was asked one day how he could write so lovingly about Paris when he'd never ever been there. He said, 'I've never been over the rainbow either!' I had the pleasure of meeting him in the seventies and he told me the story of some Broadway producer who asked him to write a song for a Broadway play called *The Great Magoo*. The producer gave him a complicated brief, he said, 'Write something that says all of us are perishable on this temporary planet.' He came up with a simple solution – 'It's Only a Paper Moon'.

| FOUR WOMEN

When you write a memoir you are forced to look back at your life. I've done that and I came to the conclusion that I was blessed from the beginning. My mother, my two sisters Nita and Adele, and Shirley; four women who make up most of my DNA. I asked my sister Adele what was the first thing that pops into her mind about mummy? She said, 'She only saw the good in everyone.' When Shirley met my mother she became her idol. She had never come across a lady who was so selfless and always smiling. Being the youngest of five I was probably spoiled the most but then again we all were. When I came home from school she would always be looking out of the window and in her warm northern accent would shout 'It's okay, Donald, there's no dogs about.' This was a time when dogs were not always on leads and she was terrified in case one bit me. I still get a little nervous around large dogs or any large animals. I can never understand how people love the idea of swimming with turtles and dolphins. It's enough to put you off the ocean.

My mother loved music and would often be heard singing songs with a gypsy flavour like 'Besame Mucho', 'Jealousy', and 'Jezebel'. She was born in the Ukraine in a town called Mariapole and my father came from Kiev. They met each other in Sunderland, and while my dad had a strange accent, a quarter Geordie,

41

three-quarters Kiev, my mother had a soothing comforting Sunderland lilt.

We all liked to perform in front of our parents. We used to sit down and my mother would introduce us – 'And now Ladies and Gentlemen please give a big hand to Michael Black.' My brother would then do some impressions of Maurice Chevalier, Edward G. Robinson and James Cagney. Next in line was 'The fabulous Nita Blackstone.' Nita was besotted with Frank Sinatra and would swoon just to hear his name. She would have a go at one of his early songs – 'Nancy (with the Laughing Face)' or 'I'll Never Smile Again' – and perform some very odd monologues with a north of England accent. My brother Cyril's party piece was an impression of Frankie Laine singing 'I'm Gonna Live Till I Die'. This was followed by Adele playing 'The Legend of the Glass Mountain' on our cigarette-stained piano. And then it came to my turn, which was usually me doing impressions of Jerry Lewis or Peter Lorre. My mother praised us all to the sky and when it came to awarding points she diplomatically gave us all ten out of ten.

My sister Nita looked after all of us and in a way was a second mother. Something happened one day that turned out to be a defining moment in my life. Nita said to me that she was going to the pictures and I said, 'Are you going to see *They Made Me a Fugitive*?' Only I'd never heard that word before and pronounced fuggertive! She burst out laughing and told everyone 'Donald said fuggertive.' I was so embarrassed by not knowing a word that from then on I would ask my teachers things like, 'What do diagnoses and ubiquitous mean?' When I met Shirley she used to test me on my vocabulary. I have a dictionary which is fifty years old that Shirley bought me and the inscription reads, 'To my darling husband, as there may be one or two words you don't know, Love Shirley.'

Adele was beautiful with her jet-black hair and blue eyes, and to this day whenever we meet she talks about those times. She has quite a few grandchildren now and she tells them endless stories about those happy days. She tells them that, 'We were poor but we always felt rich because we had the best mother in the world. None of us could do wrong in her eyes. If we had the slightest thing wrong with us – a sore throat, a cold, a spot or lump of any kind she would take us immediately to Dr. Levy. She worried so much about us all. Dr. Levy, as you can imagine, got to know us all very well.'

My father was an emotional man but he hid it very well. He was strong and had some chest expanders that only a muscleman could open. He would do this and laugh at the same time. He was strict and threatened to do this and that as fathers do. He would lose his temper and say, 'I'll take the strap to you,' and he would even undo his buckle. Thankfully, the strap never left his waist. My dad was a major smoker and he wouldn't stop. He was told that if he continued his legs would have to be amputated. He said, 'Take them off,' and they did. He was as brave as a lion and he used to say, 'I never give way,' and he never did.

MY BOYS

In the early sixties two amazing things happened to me. I was blessed with having two sons, Grant and Clive. I often joke about them saying they are the best kids money can buy. As I've said, I was on the road a lot with Matt in their early days and left the hard bits of parenthood to Shirley. I loved being young with them – Shirley said it was like having three children. When I dropped them off for school I would say to the other kids 'Do you know the exact time Elton John is coming today?' The kids were so excited that in no time the rumour was in every classroom. I did the same with Georgie Best and whoever was in the limelight at the time. I also played cowboys with them using all the dialogue I picked up from those westerns I saw at the Regal in Hackney. I would carry Clive under my arm and shout, 'I'm coming out with the kid!'

Like most families we struggled in the beginning. Our first home was a tiny flat in Highbury, we then went on to a small house in Mill Hill, and as my songs began to get recorded and I happened to write 'Born Free' we moved to a big house in Uphill Road, Mill Hill. I remember reading somewhere that the writer Graham Greene said, 'An unhappy childhood is a writer's goldmine.' In my opinion he couldn't be more wrong. We have always loved each other to bits and I know they would still think the world of me even if I had never written 'Born Free'. *your childhood, surely*

44

Unlike me and their mum, their marriages haven't always been successful, but they had funny things to say about them. Grant said, 'My marriage lasted three months but it wasn't all good.' He added 'The cake lasted longer.' Clive said about his marriage 'We were together for seven years but I don't remember breaking a mirror.'

I've always had a uniquely close relationship with my boys. We speak to each other many times a day and have always done so. Since Shirley passed Clive moved in with me for three or four nights a week, and Grant only lives next door. We have dinner together a lot and some nights my daughter-in-law, Gay-Yee, will bring my dinner to me covered in silver foil. So I am still being spoiled. Gay-Yee is a brilliant cellist and is part of the group Bond. They have been married for ten happy years. They have a son with the fancy name of Ulysses. He has to do well with a name like Ulysses Black, sounds like a future CEO of Microsoft to me.

Clive has two children with his ex-wife, Miranda. They are George and Martha. In December Martha and her partner Matt Parsons presented us with a beautiful baby girl they called Amelia Shirley. This made Clive a grandfather and me a great-grandfather which made us both happy and very sad at the same time. Shirley would have become a great-grandmother. They live in Sidcup, Kent, and they also have a dog, but thankfully a small one.

Spending so much time with Grant and Clive I have noticed something that has taken me by surprise. They seem to remember everything I've ever said to them! All my one-liners, all my early songs, they can quote them all. I'm always amazed that when I begin a story about someone I've met, they come up with the punchline well before I'm finished. This has kept me on my toes and I am constantly looking for new material so I don't come across as a repetitive old man.

They are both in the business. Grant writes terrific songs that have been recorded by Sarah Brightman, Craig David and Olly Murs. He is also in management and has written his first musical. It's called *Rehab* and by the time this book is published I hope it will be at a theatre near you.

Clive began working in music publishing, moved to records and worked his way up to becoming the youngest managing director of EMI records. He is now into music publishing, management and various aspects of the music industry. He lives in a beautiful house near Beaconsfield but I always have to warn him when I'm coming because he has a large dog that is strong enough to destroy a village. The three of us have become like the Three Musketeers – 'One for all and all for one.'

MY BROTHER MICHAEL

I've spent a lot of time with comedians over the years. My brother Michael used to book Bob Monkhouse, Bruce Forsyth, Dave Allen and Des O' Connor and they all had one thing in common: they all thought my brother was the funniest man they'd ever met who wasn't on the stage. I feel sorry for anyone who never met him. He turned exaggeration into an art form. When he managed a young singer he said, 'He sings better than Sinatra when he's got a hernia.' When he talked about one of his rich friends he would say, 'The man is worth zillionies, he's got nine swimming pools and seven live-in trainers.' When he would see a doctor he'd say, 'The man's a genius, he's got eighty-two letters after his name!'

Michael's whole life was show business and he was never really interested in anything else. He never read a book in his life. A few years ago we all went on holiday to Istanbul and we visited the famous Blue Mosque. This mosque has been there since the sixth century. While we were walking through it and soaking up the sanctified atmosphere the tour guide was telling us all about the Ottoman and Byzantine empires. Michael leaned across to me and said, 'That Joe Longthorne is unbelievable!'

He used to say to people, 'My brother can write a musical in ten minutes.'

Michael was always starstruck and movie mad. If you mentioned any old film star he would be off on a magical journey. In truth, Michael never left the playground. It wouldn't have surprised me to see his name sewn in the back of his jumper. In Michael's perfect world Bing Crosby would still be a priest, James Stewart would be the local reporter or sheriff and Deanna Durbin would still be singing from an open window.

Some years ago I wrote a song called 'One Day Soon' and it was recorded by Tom Jones. His manager was undecided if it should be his next single. It was between my song and one other. My brother said to Tom, '"One Day Soon" is in a different class to the other song, that one won't mean a light.' They decided on the other song – you may have heard of it, it was called 'Delilah'.

The best thing that happened to Michael was meeting his extraordinary wife, Julie Rogers, who was a major recording artist in the sixties. He called me up one day after Julie did a concert and I asked him how it went. He said, 'The review has just come out and the headline is Julie Rogers tore the bollocks off 'em.'

Michael died at the age of ninety-three on 1 October 2018. And even he could not exaggerate how much we all miss him. As the great Max Miller used to say, 'There'll never be another.'

SODS

What good are laurels if you can't rest on them?
Tom Lehrer

Almost fifty years ago a group of us busy songwriters got together. It was Mitch Murray's idea to form a regular gathering of songwriters who could meet two or three times a year just to stay in touch. A bunch of us met including Geoff Stephens ('Winchester Cathedral'), Barry Mason ('The Last Waltz'), Bill Martin ('Congratulations') and Les Reed ('It's Not Unusual'). We all thought this was a great idea as changing musical tastes meant that Denmark Street was no longer the meeting place it once was.

Mitch's idea was to call it the Society of Distinguished Songwriters, or SODS for short. It is still going strong all these years later. Every year there is a Ladies' Night which is one of the hottest tickets in town. The cabaret features the members singing their own songs. There is something very special about writers singing their own songs. Very few of the members are good singers, most of us can just stumble through. I often sing 'Born Free' and I'm grateful that Matt is not here to hear my version. I usually compère the Ladies' Night and it gives me the opportunity to use the comedic muscles that served me so well as a stand-up. It's all great fun. These days, as we have many older members, I like to begin the cabaret something like this:

I'd like to start by thanking all the cardiologists, urologists and proctologists for making this evening possible. We have a lot of nervous Sods here tonight and having seen the rehearsals I can understand why . . . First one out tonight is one of the best songwriters in the country. That's not only my opinion, it's his as well . . . Ladies and Gentlemen, please welcome Tony Hatch.

After Tony has sung a medley of his hits (including 'Downtown') I will say something like, 'I could listen to Tony all night and for a moment I thought I was going to have to!' I have always thought there is a correlation between jokes and lyrics. If you take any wonderful comedian and analyse what they say you realise, like wonderful lyric writers, they don't waste a syllable. For example take my old friend Henny Youngman – here's a typical one-liner from his act, 'I bought my wife a chair for her birthday, she won't plug it in.'

Now if he said, 'It was my wife's birthday the other day and I didn't know what to buy her. I ended up buying her a chair, but so far she hasn't plugged it in', he wouldn't have got nearly as many laughs.

It's the same with a song. Imagine if 'Every Time We Say Goodbye' began with, 'Every time we say goodbye I feel so lost and lonely,' instead of, 'Every time we say goodbye I die a little.' You can see there is no comparison. One is long-winded and dull and the other is crafted elegance.

You don't need many tools to be a songwriter but a rhyming dictionary is essential. A woman once saw Johnny Mercer carrying his while walking down Fifth Avenue in New York. She went up to him and said, 'So that's how you do it!' Oh, if it were only that simple. All the great wordsmiths use them and Stephen Sondheim puts it very well. He says that it saves you an enormous amount of time in dismissing ideas. For example, if you are looking for a word to rhyme with dog you look at all the og rhymes and if there's nothing there you move on to another idea quickly. I always have mine at the ready but not so much when I'm writing pop songs as there are very few clever rhymes needed these days. I have always made a list of good rhymes because you never know when they might come in handy. Some of the ones I've scribbled down over the years are: Maxine/vaccine, Connecticut/etiquette, Bombay/flambé, humour/satsuma, shyness/minus, fromage/homage, well, you get the idea. I also do this with song titles. I've been doing this automatically for so many years that when I get a melody sent to me I check if there's an idea for a song that will fit the tune. Many times there isn't one, but every now and then I stumble across a phrase I wrote down years ago and it fits the bill. I mention this because it's advice I often pass on when I'm talking to budding lyric writers. A thesaurus also comes in handy when you're searching for a synonym. Bob Monkhouse used to crack a joke about the time he worked for a thesaurus company but he was fired, dismissed, let go, discharged, sent off.

Johnny Mercer said that he once wrote the words to a Henry Mancini melody in about five minutes! He said, 'I can't take credit for that lyric – God wrote that lyric, I just took it down.' It was for a film starring Jack Lemmon. When Jack Lemmon heard it he said, 'Mercer started to sing this song and I have never been through anything like it in my life – I was wiped out – I was gone. It was one of the most thrilling moments I've ever had in this business.' The film and the song were called *The Days of Wine and Roses*.

SONGS AND SINGERS

It is the best of all trades to make songs, and the second best to sing them. **Hilaire Belloc**

Quincy Jones is nothing like Andrew Lloyd Webber, Henry Mancini was light years away from Van Morrison. Elmer Bernstein is the total opposite of Charles Aznavour. And yet, when they are at the piano these people are identical. They are all trying to find out how it goes; all in search of that elusive melody. Although I've spent years collaborating with composers, it isn't always necessary. All I need to know is how does it go? I'm just as happy receiving a CD or tape with the melody and, in truth, I don't have to spend any time with them at all. Yes, of course I have an opinion when they play me their melody. I may say 'That sounds a bit like "Over the Rainbow",' which can be pretty helpful. When I write with Van Morrison I give him a lyric and the next thing I know he's used most of it, changed a few words and then recorded it. This is heaven! I've always envied Bernie Taupin who works the same way with Elton John.

I'm often asked what I think of today's songs and singers and I'm mindful that I don't want to come across as an old curmudgeon. I miss the craft that went into those great old songs. Songs that had true rhymes and said fresh things about the human condition. Today you could rhyme 'happy' with 'lemonade' and no one would quibble. I guess that's because singers are writing songs for themselves to sing and very rarely does anyone else sing them. Also, there is very little wit in any of the songs. The world of Cole Porter is long dead I'm afraid. The generation of singers that I was raised on had something that is pretty impossible to come across these days – instant recognition. People like Sinatra, Nat King Cole, Dean Martin, Johnny Mathis, Bing Crosby, Sarah Vaughan, Ella Fitzgerald, Tony Bennett and many more had such distinctive voices you could identify them immediately. Today I really couldn't tell you who is singing. They are mostly a variation of each other. There are many fine singers but without character. And most of them sing at least five notes when one would do just fine.

I know I'm speaking of and mourning a bygone age, but songs were better then and singers had their own original personality. I dread the day when you can only acquire a Rodgers and Hart song under the hammer at Sotheby's.

> Johnny Mathis was a star athlete at George Washington High School in San Francisco. He was a high-jumper and a hurdler and he also played on the basketball team. In 1954 he enrolled at San Francisco State University on an athletic scholarship, intending to become a physical education teacher. Thankfully he was heard singing at the 440 Club by George Avakian who was an A and R man from Columbia Records. He sent a telegram to his boss in New York which read, 'I've found this phenomenal nineteen-year-old boy who could go all the way. Send blank contracts.' In 1956 he recorded 'It's Not for Me to Say', which put paid to his high-jumping ambitions.

MY FIRST SONG

A poem begins in delight and ends with wisdom.

Robert Frost

I wrote my first song when I was about fifteen. It was for a Jewish
wedding and I called it 'There's No Smoke Without Salmon'.
It went like this:

> There's no smoke without salmon
>
> There's no sorrow without soup
>
> Nothing's better than a bagel
>
> When your back begins to stoop
>
> There's no heartache without herring
>
> Chopped or pickled both are fine
>
> They did wonders for Jack Cohen
>
> And they saved Melanie Klein
>
> When things are really bad
>
> Order a salt beef sandwich
>
> But it has to be on rye
>
> When someone orders salt beef on white bread
>
> Somewhere in the world a Jew will die!
>
> There's no smoke without salmon
>
> It's a fact take it from me
>
> You'll pull through with good smoke salmon
>
> And a nice glass of lemon tea.

I always knew I wanted to do something with words, and around this time I thought I'd have a go at poetry. I read a lot of the great poets and was often disappointed at finding just a few good lines in a book that had more than five hundred pages. I feel the same way about poetry anthologies as I do about autobiographies. There seem to be acres of pretentious, flowery, mind-wandering nonsense before you read something that is insightful, truthful and illuminating. My attempts were mainly brief and pithy, which proved to me that I was more suited to writing lyrics. Here are a few of my poetic endeavours. I had this idea for a book of poems called *Men Have Feelings Too*:

> If you want to lead an easy life
> Make sure your mistress
> Wears the same perfume
> As your wife
> It's hard to write a love letter
> Full of passion, lust and rage
> When you're scared in case your fingerprints
> Are all across the page
> She knew that I was married
> But she didn't walk away
> She flirted and she pouted
> And I longed for her to stay
> We both attacked each other
> In a haze of straps and zips
> It's hard to be pragmatic
> When you're kissing eager lips
> We knew that it was stupid

> That was clearly understood
> We hurt a lot of people
> But it still felt bloody good

Well, you get the idea. I once had a chat with the poet Roger McGough who said he couldn't write lyrics because he always felt there was much more to say than what's said in a song. I've always thought exactly the opposite; the miracle of brevity has always appealed to me.

OTHER PEOPLE'S SONGS

Without music life would be a mistake.
Friedrich Nietzsche

For as far back as I can remember I have been in love with songs. Well, originally with bits of songs. When most kids of my age were collecting stamps or comic books, I would be scribbling down a line or two from a song I heard on the BBC's Light Programme. An early memory is saying to my sisters Adele and Nita how clever these lines were:

> Fish gotta swim
> Birds gotta fly
> I gotta love
> One man till I die

They're from the song 'Can't Help Loving That Man of Mine' from *Showboat* by Jerome Kern and Oscar Hammerstein. What I loved about those lines was that they were true. Fish do have to swim and birds do have to fly and it was a fresh way of saying 'I Love You' without using that overused phrase.

There are many whole songs that I love from beginning to end, and they'll help tell my story. But to start us off here are a few snippets of lines that I think are special and I wish I had written them.

THE SANEST GUY IN THE ROOM

Every time we say goodbye
I die a little
(Cole Porter)

Jolene, Jolene, Jolene, Jolene,
Please don't take him just because you can
(Dolly Parton)

I could have told you Vincent
This world was never meant for one as beautiful as you.
(Don McLean)

Something's lost and something's gained
In living every day
(Joni Mitchell)

They'll never believe me, they'll never believe me
That from this great big world you've chosen me
(Jerome Kern/Herbert Reynolds)

I took my troubles down to Madam Ruth
You know that gypsy with the gold-capped tooth
She's got a pad down on Thirty-Fourth and Vine
Sellin' little bottles of Love Potion Number Nine
(Jerry Lieber/Mike Stoller)

I shoulda changed that stupid lock
I shoulda made you leave your key
If I'd have known for just one second
You'd be back to bother me
(Ferrin/Pakaris)

Although I was more or less raised on the Great American Songbook, I have always tried to keep up with contemporary songwriters. I think it is just as difficult to write a song for Taylor Swift or Britney Spears as it is to write a song for a Broadway show. It's an entirely different craft but equally challenging. I also like to listen to jazz, country music and folk music. As Duke Ellington said, 'There's only two kinds of music – good and bad.'

My love of the Great American Songbook has been a great asset because as a result I have my own BBC show on Radio Two. About seven years ago the late and much respected broadcaster David Jacobs heard me when I stood in for Elaine Paige. He told the BBC people that he thought I did a great job and recommended me to take over his slot when he retired. I had done quite a bit of radio work before but this was a chance to play anything I wanted and to tell stories about the many talented and starry people I've met over the years. Hosting this show is a labour of love and has proved a winner, particularly with people of my generation who were raised listening to Frank Sinatra, Ella Fitzgerald, Johnny Mathis, Tony Bennett and the rest. The format is quite simple: I play great songs by great singers. You rarely hear these stars on the radio today and the letters I get from listeners prove that there is still a demand for them. I had a letter recently from a lady who said, 'When I listen to your show and all those wonderful artists and songs, for one hour a week I am young again.'

> In William Zinsser's book *Easy to Remember*, he writes eloquently about what happens when he's at the piano and plays a Gershwin song, or a Rodgers and Hart or Cole Porter song. He says he looks at the people in the room and their faces change; the aches and worries drop away. Watching them, he says, reminds him that pianists who play these songs end up doing more than they signed up to do. The songs themselves provide solace and release and joy and the consolations of memory. I'm sure he's right. I know I feel better when I hear songs like 'Embraceable You' or 'The Way You Look Tonight'.

Here are a couple of favourites of mine and my listeners:

'The Way You Look Tonight'
This just might be my favourite song of all time. It was written for a film called *Swing Time* starring Fred Astaire and Ginger Rogers. It won an Oscar for the best song in a motion picture in 1936. It has a beautiful haunting melody and the lyric is so truthful. Whenever any of us feel down we pull ourselves together by thinking of the person we love and that thought chases the blues away. This also happens to be a lot of people's favourite song! I remember Jule Styne singing its praises and John Barry thought it was one of Kern's best melodies. I read a lovely story about a father in Cincinnati whose daughter was getting married and he was going crazy with worry about what to say in his wedding speech. He wrote many versions and wasn't happy with any of them. Then one day he heard Sinatra sing this song and he thought that it said exactly what he would be feeling on the wedding day. When the time came for his speech, he got up and recited this lyric to a teary-eyed audience:

Some day, when I'm awfully low

When the world is cold

I will feel a glow just thinking of you

And the way you look tonight

Yes you're lovely, with your smile so warm

And your cheek so soft

There is nothing for me but to love you

Just the way you look tonight

With each word your tenderness grows

Tearing my fears apart

And that laugh that wrinkles your nose

Touches my foolish heart

Lovely . . . never ever change

Keep that breathless charm

Won't you please arrange? Cause I love you

Just the way you look tonight

'As Time Goes By'

Bruce Springsteen once remarked that people don't go to see him,
they go to see themselves. I think that's a very true observation.
Seeing a big star singing songs that take you back to happy or
deeply remembered days is the real reason to buy the ticket
or play the record. That is what happens to me every time I hear
'As Time Goes By'. It was written by a man hardly anyone has
ever heard of – Herman Hupfeld. He wrote it for a failed musical
called *Everybody's Welcome* in 1931. It's a complicated story of
how it wound up in the film *Casablanca*. In short, the film
company owned the music publishing rights and they didn't have
to pay anything to use it in the picture. Whenever *Casablanca*

comes on television, in my mind I am nowhere near Casablanca. I'm at the Pavilion Cinema in Mare Street, Hackney, with my mum and dad, my brothers Michael and Cyril and my sisters Nita and Adele. We are all eating a Wall's ice cream (which cost fourpence each), and we are all carried away by the story, the music and the faces of Humphrey Bogart and Ingrid Bergman. We are also thinking of the chips we will be eating at Joe's Fish Shop after the film. The song has stayed with me ever since I heard it:

> Moonlight and love songs
> Never out of date
> Hearts full of passion
> Jealousy and hate
> Woman needs man
> And man must have his mate
> That no one can deny

There, once again, is that universal truth, so important in a song. The opening line of the song also grabs you and urges you to tune into the rest of it:

> You must remember this . . .

When I'm asked about my favourite songs of the ones I've written I automatically go back to where they were written and what I was staring at. 'Love Changes Everything' conjures up a delightful walk around Cap Ferrat. 'Thunderball' reminds me of our first flat in Highbury, North London, overlooking a noisy railway

62

station. This was a far cry from 'Sunset Boulevard' which was written by the pool of the grand Bel Air Hotel with my collaborator Christopher Hampton. What has never changed is the endless pursuit of finding something fresh to say about feelings, and love in particular. As the song says:

> The fundamental things apply
> As time goes by.

Whenever I meet Liza Minnelli I am amazed at her knowledge of old songs. She told me that some people collect coins or stamps but she's always collected songs. She said that everything she's ever felt had been written in a song. She added, 'Songs punctuate your emotions throughout your life.'

EVERYTHING MUST CHANGE

'It will always be this way' is the assumption that dominates a happy life. My mother will always be in the kitchen singing 'Besame Mucho', my father will always go, once a week, to the Hackney Wick Dog Track, my brother Michael will be doing his impression of Edward G Robinson for ever, my sister Nita will always be taking me to the pictures, my brother Cyril will never stop challenging anyone to an arm wrestle and my sister Adele will stay in love with Gregory Peck.

'It will always be this way' – that blind faith in things staying as they are continues. My son Grant will always get sick on top of buses, my other son Clive will always collect stamps and my wife Shirley will always close her eyes when she listens to my lyrics.

My mother is no longer here to sing 'Besame Mucho', my father has gone to his race track in the sky. My brother Michael is no longer here; maybe he's actually playing poker with Edward G. Robinson. Nita recently turned ninety, Cyril is eighty-four and Adele is now eighty-two and I'm not far behind. Grant and Clive are in their fifties and Shirley, the love of my life, must be in the place where good people go.

The feeling of 'nothing will change' is a self-induced safety blanket that shields us from the harsh reality of life. Most emotions have been captured in a song and so has this one. Bernard

Ighner was an American Jazz singer and songwriter and close friend of Quincy Jones. He wrote a beautiful song about this called 'Everything Must Change'. It's more of a poem than a song and has been recorded by many people including Barbra Streisand and Nina Simone.

> Everything must change
> Nothing stays the same
> Everyone will change
> No one stays the same
> There are not many things in life
> You can be sure of
> Except rain comes from the clouds
> The sun lights up the sky
> And hummingbirds do fly

Since I lost Shirley on 7 March 2018, the enormity of grief has reshaped my life. I'm not speaking in terms of those bumper-sticker slogans – 'Seize the Day' or 'One Day at a Time' – it's much deeper and wider than that. Disappointments have taken on a different meaning. When you've somehow managed to live through an emotional tsunami, dashed hopes become merely an April shower. On the other hand pleasant news becomes exhilarating. For eighteen months I felt that I was paying the price for being so happy for so long. Thankfully my dark days are slowly turning into dark moments. All of us will suffer the agony of devastating grief at some point, but hopefully, as the songs says, 'Everything must change', nothing stays the same.

MY BUCKET LIST

I recently had a visit from my friend and neighbour the television presenter Angela Rippon.

She was saying that she wants to start slowing down as there's so much she wants do, so many places she wants to see. She rattled off about a dozen faraway places with strange-sounding names. I told her that I have no desire to go anywhere. In fact once I thought about it I realised there is nothing on my bucket list. I don't want to go sky diving, learn to play an instrument, see the Taj Mahal, walk along the Great Wall of China, snorkel at the Great Barrier Reef, take an African safari or wrap a snake around my neck. I also don't want to own anything like a yacht, a plane, a Porsche or a Rolex.

I am very content to stay put and live a simple, uncomplicated and unadventurous life. I am in favour of progress, but if I'm honest it isn't only songs that were better when I was growing up. I still haven't forgiven the Post Office for making us dial numbers only when making a phone call. They took all the poetry and romance out of it. You now dial 629 when it used to be MAYfair. It was so much easier to remember a number when there were fewer of them. Many of us of a certain age remember with nostalgic delight:

COVent Garden, JUNiper, WATerloo and COPpermill

CHErrywood and KNIghtsbridge, IVAnhoe and SUNny Hill

KENsington TRAfalgar, TEMplebar and LONdon Wall

SEVenkings and GULliver, We've even lost WHItehall

MAIdaVale, SWIss Cottage, GIPsy Hill, TATe Gallery,

SILverthorn and BLUebell, TURnham Green and CANonbury

So many numbers in my head

I think I'll write a note instead

I feel pretty much the same about restaurants. I have no wish to savour Heston Blumenthal's creative dishes of snail porridge or bacon and egg ice cream. Call me old-fashioned but I like to eat food I understand. Michael Winner once said of me that Don Black requires two things from restaurants: they have to be cheap and cheerful! The truth is I have a few places I go to all the time as it annoys me to waste an evening on small portions that are served on big white plates.

I've gone off going to see films as often as I used to. I don't like to see things that can't happen. The minute I see a man fly I'm out of there. I'd much rather stay home and watch all the great entertainers and comedians on YouTube. If I was still a comic all the material is there for the stealing, er, I mean taking. A few years ago, newspapers and magazines used to feature a questionnaire that was supposed to reveal little-known facts about a particular personality. I answered a bunch of them:

Q Which word or phrase do you most overuse?

A What does it all mean?

Q What is your greatest regret?
A Not cashing in on my physique.

Q How do you relax?
A Playing snooker.

Q What single thing would improve your way of life?
A Wings.

Q What keeps you awake at night?
A Thinking about how much longer *The Mousetrap* can keep running.

Q Do you believe in life after death?
A From time to time.

Q How would you like to be remembered?
A As a spiritual icon.

Q What is the most important lesson life has taught you?
A Be yourself.

Q What is your favourite smell?
A Chicken soup.

Q What is your favourite word?
A Buxom.

Q What is your favourite journey?
A A walk to the RAC Club through Holland Park, Hyde Park and Green Park.

Q What trait do you most deplore in others?
A Long-windedness.

Q What is your favourite fantasy?

A It's hazy but it includes a blues singer, sniffer dogs and Branston Pickles.

Q For what cause would you die?

A The continuance of the Eurovision Song Contest.

Q What is your idea of perfect happiness?

A Beating Ronnie O'Sullivan in a game of snooker.

Q Which historical figure do you most identify with?

A Delilah. It's a long story.

Q What do you consider the most overrated virtue?

A Self-denial.

Q What was your most embarrassing moment?

A Meeting Little Richard and saying Hello Little.

Q What makes you depressed?

A Talking to piano tuners.

Q What is your most unappealing habit?

A Not listening.

Q What is your greatest fear?

A Climbing a ladder.

Q What do you dislike about yourself?

A I get bored easily.

Q What is the nastiest thing anyone has ever said to you?

A In the middle of my act one night when everything was going great and people were laughing and cheering, I overheard someone say, 'How about this kid, he believes us.'

Q Can you tell us one thing people don't know about you?

A I don't play an instrument.

Q What drives you mad?

A People asking me if I'm still writing or have I retired? I like to remind them that when Sir John Gielgud was ninety-two he changed agents.

Q What is your favourite film?

A *Atlantic City* starring Burt Lancaster.

Q Which living person do you most admire and why?

A My wife Shirley. She doesn't know the meaning of the word moody.

MUSICALS

My first failed musical, the first of many, was called *Maybe That's Your Problem*. The great Elaine Paige was in it and it ran at the Roundhouse Theatre in Camden Town. It was a peculiar story about a young man who got overexcited around girls. Well, to be more precise he suffered from premature ejaculation. Ironically, the show didn't last long either! However, John Barry came to see it and brought with him Alan Jay Lerner, who was a hero of mine. When the show finished Alan came over to me and quoted a line of lyric that I wrote in one of the songs – 'While I've got the stamina to cram in a few dreams'. He put his arm around me and said, 'Dear Boy, stamina and cramina, bloody brilliant!' Those few words from this theatrical giant spurred me on to keep going.

Alan was a short, dapper man who wore bow ties and said 'Dear Boy' a lot! 'Dear Boy' was usually followed by some words of wisdom, as in 'Dear Boy, always remember that in the whole world there's never been a statue erected to a critic' or 'Dear Boy, always remember that theatre owners are only landlords!' or 'Dear Boy, do you realise that between me and Rex Harrison we have had fourteen wives . . . we've supported more women than Playtex!'

I eventually got to know Alan well and we used to meet for lunch regularly at a restaurant in Wilton Street. He was charming and witty. One of my prize possessions is his autobiography. It is called *The Street Where I Live*, and in it he inscribed the words, 'How can one lyric writer love another one.' Once, when he came back from a holiday in Capri with his last wife Liz Robertson, I asked him if he had a good time. He said he had a great time but everywhere he went he kept hearing Stephen Sondheim songs. He then paused and said 'Funny how a little thing like that can ruin your holiday.'

It was on *Maybe That's Your Problem* that I got my first glimpse of the tension you can come across in a rehearsal room. The book writer was Lionel Chetwynd and one day after a creative discussion he kicked a chair over. The orchestrator was John Cameron who went on to orchestrate *Les Misérables*. After another creative discussion he tossed his scores in the air. When, for the song 'There's No Business Like Show Business', Irving Berlin came up with the line, 'Everything about it is appealing', I think he was wrong.

We all thought, wrongly, that the story of *Maybe That's Your Problem* was a good idea. The reason was that it came out around the time Philip Roth's *Portnoy's Complaint* was sweeping the world. This book sparked a storm of controversy over its explicit and candid treatment of sexuality. Alan Jay Lerner said we should have called our show *Shortcomings*!

After a very few brief encounters our main character, Marvin Gold, is left alone on stage to sing 'Something Must Have Happened':

> Whenever there's a pretty girl
> Standing by my side

MUSICALS

All I have to do is hold her hand
And I'm completely satisfied
How embarrassing this situation
It's making me quite sick
If a lady wants to love me
She better be quick

It isn't natural
There must be a reason why
If I delve into my childhood
I might find the answer
So I'll try

Something must have happened
Wish I could remember what
Then maybe I can solve
This awful problem that I've got
There's nothing strange about the life I led
Each night Aunt Sadie
Would tuck me in bed
I remember on some mornings
Auntie's face was scarlet red
(spoken) Oh no!
But something must have happened
Way back somewhere in my youth
If I can turn the clock back
I might come across the truth
I even get excited when a lady blows a kiss
I can't bear to think of all those

THE SANEST GUY IN THE ROOM

Delicious sins I've missed

Women are so demanding

They're hard to satisfy

They still expect you to love them

After three minutes have gone by

But the women of today

Would be in a state

On that very merry day

When Marvin Gold

Starts to recuperate.

BILLY

This musical based on the book and film of *Billy Liar* by Keith Waterhouse and Willis Hall was a dream project. It was John Barry's idea and it was also his idea to get Dick Clement and Ian La Frenais to adapt it as a musical. It starred Michael Crawford and Elaine Paige and ran for almost three years at London's Theatre Royal, Drury Lane. It opened my eyes to a whole new world where you could write about all kinds of things, as opposed to pop songs where you are limited to catchy hooks. It was a critical and commercial success and proved life-changing for me. I was hooked on musicals. Of course, there were a few dramas; Michael Crawford broke his arm while we were previewing the show in Manchester. There were also quite a few creative differences. Michael ad-libbed a lot and this didn't go down well with Dick and Ian. Thankfully, for me, it's impossible to ad-lib lyrics! One memorable day when Michael was being unpleasant to our director, Patrick Garland, during rehearsals, John Barry shouted out to him not to be such an idiot. Michael replied, 'Don't talk to me like that, don't you realise how important I am to this production?' John then replied loudly 'If you're so important why am I telling you to fuck off?' I think Michael did just that for a few days.

For an opening night present John gave Michael a gold watch which he bought at the exclusive Asprey's store in Bond Street.

He explained to the elegantly tailored salesman that it was for Michael Crawford and he would like to engrave some words on the back of the watch. He said, 'I would like it to read "Cunt, thank you for Billy."' The salesman's eyes widened. Clearly this was not a request Asprey's had encountered before. '"Cunt", sir?' John began to spell it. 'Yes, "cunt" C . . . U . . . ' 'I do know how to spell it sir, thank you, sir.'

When Michael received the gift he saw the funny side of it and tells the story to this day.

The big song from the show was 'Some of Us Belong to the Stars'.

> Some of us belong to the stars
> And that is where I'm going
> I will fly all over the sky
> And I won't need a Boeing
> Most people stay and battle on
> With their boredom
> But what's the sense in dreaming dreams
> If you hoard 'em
> It won't be long before
> I say my ta ta's
> I belong to the stars
>
> Some of us belong to the stars
> Up there is where you'll find me
> If you wanna come for the ride
> Then form a queue behind me
> Soon I'll be wallowing in all of life's riches

BILLY

I'm gonna carve myself some crater-like niches
You better go rehearse your hip hip hoorahs
I belong to the stars

Some of us belong to the stars
There's followers and leaders
Some of us are born to be great
And some are born conceders
So I will go wherever winners assemble
From now on the world won't spin
It will tremble
I'll soon be passing round the Cuban cigars
I belong to the stars

Some of us belong to the stars,
We fly around in orbit
We soak up the wisdom of life
While others can't absorb it
I'll hang my hat in every part of the atlas
Most of the time I will be
Hopelessly hatless
You must come visit one of my Shangri-Las
I belong to the stars
I belong to the stars

One thing I've noticed on opening nights is the way big stars and producers have developed a talent for avoiding eye contact with lesser mortals, in much the same way as a woman avoids an unflattering mirror.

SOME YOU WIN, SOME YOU LOSE

If people don't want to see a show nothing will stop them.
Sol Hurok

Alan Jay Lerner had enormous success with *My Fair Lady*, *Camelot*, *Paint Your Wagon* and *Gigi* but he also had a bunch of humiliating failures – *Dance a Little Closer*, *Carmelina*, *Lolita*, *Coco* and *1600 Pennsylvania Avenue*. It may surprise you to learn that Oscar Hammerstein also had a heap of musical flops. He followed his seminal hit *Oklahoma!* with these forgotten efforts: *Sunny River*, *Very Warm for May*, *Three Sisters* and *Free for All*. When you reckon that every musical in those days took two or three years to produce, the amount of time spent on creating flops was nothing short of heartbreaking. And some of the people who go to a show they haven't enjoyed can be so insensitive to the creators of that show. You have no idea how hurtful and devastating a mere comment of disapproval can be.

Stephen Sondheim told a friend of mine exactly what he expects from friends on one of his opening nights. It was something like this:

> Once a creation has been put into the world, you have only one responsibility to the creator: be supportive. Support is not about showing how clever you are, how observant of some flaw, how incisive in your criticism.

78

If you come to my show and you see me afterwards, say only this: 'I loved it.' It doesn't matter what you really felt. What I need at that moment is to know that you care enough about me and the work I do to tell me that you loved it. Not 'in spite of its flaws'. But simply, plainly, 'I loved it'. If you can't say that, don't come backstage, don't find me in the lobby, just go home, and either write me a nice email or don't. Say all the catty, bitchy things you want to say to your friend, your neighbour, the internet. Maybe next week, maybe next year, maybe someday down the line I'll be ready to hear what you have to say, but at that moment, that face-to-face moment after I have unveiled some part of my soul, however small to you: that is the most vulnerable moment in any artist's life. I beg you, plead with you, not to tell me what you really thought, what you actually, honestly, believed. You must tell me 'I loved it'. That moment must be respected.

It would appear that playwright George Kaufman was right when he said, 'For anyone working in the theatre disappointment is inevitable.'

Jerry Bock and Sheldon Harnick had one of the biggest ever Broadway hits when they wrote *Fiddler on the Roof*. They then wrote quite a few shows that didn't do so well. Jerry Bock said a few years ago that, 'The success of *Fiddler* has been so gratifying but along with its success has come no insight of how to do it again.'

Speaking of failure, I have many books on my shelves with the entire catalogues of Johnny Mercer, Frank Loesser, Ira Gershwin,

Rodgers and Hart, Noël Coward, etc. In each book there are roughly 1,500 songs but nobody's heard of more than about fifty of them.

Marvin Hamlisch told me he once had a big flop musical on Broadway and the next day he tried to get a taxi outside his Park Avenue apartment. None of them stopped. He said to himself 'They must have read the reviews.'

I adored my collaboration with Marvin. We worked together on *The Goodbye Girl* when it came to the West End. He was so full of life, I used to call him the Jewish blowtorch. He was the funniest composer I've ever met; he had a limitless number of jokes. This was his favourite one and he told it to me about twenty times: Three Jewish men were deciding what to buy a boy for his bar mitzvah. The first man says, 'I'm going to buy him a leather-bound book of the Old Testament.' The second man says, 'I've thought a lot about this and I'm going to buy him a beautiful Jewish scroll in Hebrew.' The third man says, 'I'm going to buy the kid an umbrella.' 'Why an umbrella?' the other two say. The third man replies, 'I'd like to buy something he'll open.'

I remember talking to Alan Jay Lerner and his then wife Liz Robertson about Alan's new Broadway show called *Dance a Little Closer*. He had written it with the wonderful composer Charles Strouse and he was really excited about it as he jetted off to New York. Unfortunately the show lasted just one night. Alan sent me a letter saying, 'Liz and I will be home about a year earlier than expected. Heigh ho.'

| COLLABORATION

I am a huge fan of the writer Mark Steyn. He is a political commentator but also the world's leading authority on songwriters and what makes them tick. He said of me: 'If you can't work with Don, you can't work with anyone. He suffers the crippling disadvantage in showbusiness of being almost weirdly normal. At any read-through or rehearsal, he's the sanest guy in the room.' When I first read that I didn't know if it was a compliment or not, but I have to admit it is pretty accurate. The writer David Quantick once said, 'Don has been at the epicentre of the most glamorous projects in movie and musical history, yet he remains the same Don Black he used to be when he was the teaboy at the *New Musical Express.*'

I have worked with loads of sensitive, moody, volatile egomaniacs and emotionally disturbed people, but somehow I have managed to let their tantrums go in one ear and out the other. My mother used to say to me, 'As long as we're all well that's all that's important.' Thankfully that philosophy has been my bedrock throughout my whole life. Dedication and detachment are the best two words I can think of to describe how I've lived my life. I am 100 per cent dedicated to every project I enter into but I also do my best to be 100 per cent detached when I get home. If I am the sanest guy in the room, I can thank my wonderful family for that. After a long and difficult day working on a musical a lot of creative people will go out and smoke, drink or snort something. It has always been a cup of tea in the kitchen with Shirley that did more for me than all the Valium in Boots.

I'm pleased to say that I've never had an argument with any of my many collaborators, although I did once have a few words with Charles Aznavour. He had a huge hit in France with a song called 'La Mama'. I was asked to write an English lyric to it. It's a very sad song about a son whose mother has passed away and it tells the story of how he vows to take responsibility for bringing up the family. Charles liked what I did but thought it could be sadder. He said that in French the son is holding his mother's cold dead hand while he is singing. I said that wouldn't work in English. He then told me you can sing anything in English, as you can in French. I tried to explain that you can't sing a word like divorce or alimony in a ballad in English. We argued about this for some time because his songs are about real-life domestic issues and his audience expects and will accept this from him. Jean Cocteau once said, 'Despair wasn't popular until Charles Aznavour'. I couldn't convince him and the song became successful; it was even performed by his favourite artist Ray Charles. When I met him later I said to him, 'I've come up with a word that even you wouldn't put in a song.' 'What is it?' he said. I said, 'Catheter.' He laughed.

'For Mama'

She said, my son I beg of you

I have a wish that must come true

The last thing you can do

For Mama

Please promise me

That you will stay

And take my place

While I'm away

And give the children

Love each day

I had to cry

What could I say

How hard I tried to find a word

I prayed she wouldn't see my cry

So much to say that should be heard

But only time to say goodbye

To Mama

They say in time you will forget

Yet still today my eyes are wet

I tell myself to smile

For Mama

Now soon there'll be another spring

And I will start remembering

The way she loved to hear us sing

Her favourite song 'Ave Maria'

Ave Maria

The children all have grown up now

THE SANEST GUY IN THE ROOM

I kept my promise to mama

I cannot guide them any more

I've done my best all for mama

Ave Maria

Still this seems

So very small

For all she did for me.

I remember sitting next to the writer Paul Williams at an Oscar ceremony in 1976. I was nominated for a song I wrote with Henry Mancini for the film *The Pink Panther Strikes Again* and he was nominated for 'Evergreen', the song he wrote with Barbra Streisand for the film *A Star Is Born*. Paul and Barbra won the Oscar that night and I asked Paul, who didn't look that happy, 'What was it like working with Barbra?' and he said, 'It was like having a picnic on a runway.'

FAME

Fame if you win it
Comes and goes in a minute
Where is the real stuff in life to cling to?
(**Betty Comden** and **Adolph Green**)

A lot of people are bothered about fame but I've always cherished my anonymity. It's nice, every now and again, to be recognised in the park or on a bus or by a cab driver, but to be more famous than that has never been a desire of mine. To walk down a street with Andrew Lloyd Webber can be a scary experience. His face is so well known and heads turn all the time. There is something appealing to me about the witness protection scheme.

One of the most successful songwriters of all time was Harry Warren. Not many people have even heard of him but he wrote dozens of hit songs: 'That's Amore', '42nd Street', 'Lullaby of Broadway', 'The More I See You', 'Chatanooga Choo-choo', 'September in the Rain', 'Lulu's Back in Town', 'Jeepers Creepers', 'You Must Have Been a Beautiful Baby' and lots more. He said the reason he isn't well known is because he was a very happily married man and never once went to a Hollywood party.

THUNDERBALL

The first thing I did was to look up the word thunderball in the dictionary and it wasn't there. All I had to go on was that I knew James Bond was regarded as a man's man. When I came up with the first line, 'He always runs while others walk', the rest of the song came quickly. We always wanted Tom Jones to sing it because he was a man's man and had such a muscular voice. It has often been said that Tom fainted when he sang the last note and it's true. It wasn't actually a proper faint, more of a brain rush woozy thing that he soon got over. I had no idea that this association with a Bond film would be such a boost to my career. There are millions of Bond fans around the world who are obsessed with Bond. John Barry went on to receive five Oscars but it's the Bond franchise that he's most known for.

People often ask me how I go about writing a Bond song. Well, I always believe it should be provocative, seductive and have the whiff of the boudoir about it. There should also be the lure of the forbidden, a kind of theatrical vulgarity as you are drawn into Bond's mysterious world. I also think that Tom or Shirley Bassey should sing them all! As Terry Wogan used to say 'They don't sing songs, they bite lumps out of them.'

Over the years the Bond theme songs have changed considerably. All the songs I've written for the Bond films have been done in the old-fashioned way. John Barry was not a performer so he couldn't sing them. Also, David Arnold doesn't sing, although he should. More about him later. This meant that the focus was always on getting the song right and worrying about who would sing it later. I'm not sure when it happened but this much sought-after gig was handed over to the most popular pop group or artist at the time. It was a kind of guarantee that the song would sell and every time it was played on the radio it would be an enormous promotional tool for the film. This promotion might have worked but often the songs haven't felt integral to the mood of the picture.

John wasn't happy collaborating with what he called 'pop people'. When he worked on *The Living Daylights* with the Norwegian group A-ha, he said it was like playing table tennis with four balls.

> He always runs while others walk
> He acts while other men just talk
> He looks at this world and wants it all
> So he strikes like Thunderball
>
> He knows the meaning of success
> His needs are more so he gives less
> They call him the winner who takes all
> And he strikes like Thunderball
>
> Any woman he wants he'll get
> He will break any heart without regret
> His days of asking are all gone
> His fight goes on and on and on
> But he thinks that the fight is worth it all
> So he strikes like Thunderball

TOM JONES

One of my most embarrassing moments occurred during an evening I spent with Tom Jones. We were both staying at the Continental Hyatt House on Sunset Boulevard. Tom's agent at that time was a man called Lloyd Greenfield, who also looked after Liberace. Lloyd wanted Tom to go to West Covina to see Liberace in concert. This did not appeal to Tom at all and he begged me to go with him to keep him company. It took a few hours to get there and as soon as Liberace came on and started his flowery way of playing I could see Tom was finding it painful. Then Liberace said he wanted to introduce, 'two people who have come from far away to be here tonight. The Oscar-winning lyricist Don Black. I'll be playing his song "Born Free" later, and the great singing star whose song "It's Not Unusual" is a hit all over the world, Tom Jones.'

We took a bow and a few minutes later Tom said to me, 'I can't take any more of this, let's go to the bar.' We waited for an opportune moment and scooted quickly to the bar where Tom had a few screwdrivers. After some time I said to Tom, 'We better get back, the show will soon be over.' But as we were coming out of the bar we heard Liberace saying, 'I want to thank Don Black and Tom Jones for being here tonight.' A spotlight highlighted two empty seats. I still get night sweats about that moment.

top row third from right. *(author's collection)*

(left) Me in my stand-up days. *(author's collection)*

(above) A poster from my days as a comedian. I think I was ahead of my time . . . *(author's collection)*

Tom had a very funny road manager. He was single, loved women and never stopped swearing. One day he came up to me and said, 'What a effing night I had last night! I met this effing bird who had the best effing tits and arse I've ever effing seen. We had a few effing drinks and I took her up to my effing room, took her effing clothes off, slung her on the effing bed and intimacy occurred!'

ANDREW LLOYD WEBBER

In the theatre it's not enough to give people something they
know, you have to give them something they can't even
imagine. **Hal Prince**

There is a side to Andrew Lloyd Webber that not many people
are aware of. There's something almost of the naughty
schoolboy about him. After we finished writing the musical
Aspects of Love, he said to me, 'I think it might be a good idea to
ask a few mates over to hear the score.' I said, 'Who are you
thinking of?' He thought a bit and said, 'Margaret Thatcher,
Michael Heseltine, Geoffrey Howe, John Selwyn Gummer, John
Major, David Frost . . . ' I said, 'What good will that do?' and he
said, 'Well at least we'll find out what Joe Public thinks of it.'

I also remember him busily scribbling a note one time we were
flying to New York on Concorde. I still have that note. It was to
Jimmy Savile (long before he was revealed as an evil monster), C/O
Jim'll Fix It, and it went something like this: Dear Jimmy, I am
supposed to be one of the world's leading composers and I am
flying with one of the world's leading lyric writers to New York. It is
most embarrassing that neither of us has any of our songs featured
in the in-flight entertainment on board the plane. Do you think you
could fix it that one or two of our efforts could be featured on our
return journey? Sincerely Andrew Lloyd Webber. I still read that
note from time to time to remind myself of such carefree pleasures.

My parents
Betsy and Morris
Blackstone with
my sister Nita in
the background
trying to get in
on it. *(author's
collection)*

School picture.

Me with my sister Adele.
(author's collection)

My pare
(author's c

Me and Matt Monro on our first trip to New York. *(author's collection)*

NME days with Nat King Cole and journalist Mike Butcher. *(author's collection)*

Me with Matt Monro and John Barry
at the 'Born Free' session.
(author's collection)

The night that changed my life . . .
(author's collection)

Another shot of me and Dean Martin.
(author's collection)

John Barry, Tom Jones and me at the 'Thunderball' session. *(author's collection)*

John Barry in those 'Diamonds Are Forever' days. *(author's collection)*

'The name's Black, Don Black.'

'You're only supposed to blow the bloody doors off!' *(Paramount/Oakhuyrst Productions/Kobal/Shutterstock)*

John Wayne in *True Grit*. Not a great title for a song. *(Moviestore/Shutterstock)*

Billy: my West End debut as a lyricist. *(Trinity Mirror/Mirrorpix/Alamy Stock Photo)*

Those *Tell Me on a Sunday* days . . . *(Dezo Hoffman/Shutterstock)*

A year or so ago Andrew was still thinking of notes to send when he came up with the hilarious idea of dropping a line to Nicholas Hytner (who was then running the National Theatre). The note would have more or less said:

Dear Nick,

I have recently met a Texan billionaire who is keen to invest around 50 million dollars in the arts. After many meetings with this eccentric man I have convinced him to donate this large amount of money to the National Theatre. He asks for very little in return and I do hope you can agree to his request. He would like to change the name of the Olivier Theatre to The Jim Davidson.

Sincerely,
Andrew

Andrew has talked to me about his epiphany moment, when he realised that anything was possible in the theatre. He went to a panto in Bristol when he was about seven. It was *Aladdin*, and during the show the genie said to Aladdin, 'You can have one wish.' He thought about it and said, 'I would love to hear Alma Cogan sing "Sugar in the morning, sugar in the evening, sugar at suppertime."' Lo and behold it came to be!

The Tom Jones/Liberace moment was excruciating, but there was a moment with Andrew which was thrilling. Andrew had an apartment on the sixtieth floor of Trump Tower in New York and he invited some of his 'mates' over including Donald Trump and Steven Spielberg. Andrew introduced me to Steven and when he said, 'Steven, do you know Don Black?' Steven blurted out, 'You're not THE Don Black who wrote my favourite James Bond theme?' I was shocked that he had even heard of me, but then he went on about the marriage of Maurice Binder's title sequence and the lyrics to 'Diamonds Are Forever' being just 'perfect'. He didn't stop there, he continued with, 'The way the light catches the diamond on the word "lustre" is masterful. A moment to cherish.'

COLLABORATION REVISITED

Billy Wilder has described the perfect recipe for a good collaboration: 'Work with someone you respect who thinks differently from you.' Andrew, Christopher Hampton and myself are three very different types. However, a bit of each of us has rubbed off on the others. For instance Christopher doesn't drive and spends a fortune on taxis. I on the other hand am a big fan of public transport. Since working with me and collecting his OAP's Freedom Pass he is now a regular user of the underground. Christopher is one of the most well-read people I've ever met and as a result of our close collaboration I can now quote the odd line by Voltaire or Goethe.

Working with Andrew for so many years I now know a bit about Pre-Raphaelite art, and I notice a subtle change in his speaking patterns since working with a Jewish lyricist. For example he used to say, 'It's terrible weather outside,' now he is more likely to say, 'I can't believe the weather we're having.'

In 1926 George and Ira Gershwin were writing the musical *Oh, Kay!* when Ira was rushed into hospital for an appendix operation. He stayed in hospital for six weeks and had appalling deadlines to finish the score. His friend, the lyricist Howard Dietz, offered to help and came up with some suggestions for song titles. 'Someone to Watch Over Me' is one of my favourite Ira Gershwin lyrics but the title was Howard Dietz's.

ROOM 101

I may be the sanest guy in the room but I do get riled by silly, annoying things. I think a fortune could be raised simply for the poor of Africa if the judges of *Strictly Come Dancing* and *The X Factor* paid a pound for every time they said the word 'Amazing!' The same could be said of the hearty canned laughter that is added after every lame joke on *Have I Got News For You*.

If I ever get invited on the television programme *Room 101*, this would be the first thing I'd chuck into it – those big, boring, heavy, over-detailed books about musicals. Do we really care if a verse of a song was cut from a try-out in Boston and later reinstated when the show opened in San Diego? Who can possibly be interested in the minor revisions or cast changes when a show was being mounted in Sarasota? This exhaustive cataloguing of insignificant incidents makes for a very dull and teeth-grinding read.

I would also forbid the use of Latin words for flowers and plants. Is there anything more pretentious than when gardening pundits on television talk about *Bellis perennis* when they could say daisy, or *Hyacinthoides non-scripta* when they could just say bluebell?

One more thing that drives me crazy is *Desert Island Discs*. I believe that the 'castaway' too often chooses the records to impress the listeners. I have a friend who is a rock and roll fanatic; when he's in his car all he ever plays are records by Little Richard, Elvis Presley, Jerry Lee Lewis, Chuck Berry etc. And yet when he was a guest on the show he went for Bach, Kurt Weill and Manuel de Falla. As they say across the pond, 'Go figure.'

With this in mind I do not intend to go through all my shows with minute and forensic detail. I'll tell you about some of the memories that have stayed with me, but if you want to know what colour shoes Glenn Close had on when she auditioned for *Sunset Boulevard* I'm afraid you've picked up the wrong book.

THE OTHER DON BLACK

On a strictly personal note, I am bombarded on a daily basis with someone who has the same name as me. I get frequent Google Alerts about the other Don Black. He happens to be an American white supremacist and founder of the anti-Semitic, neo-Nazi, Holocaust-denial and racist Stormfront internet-forum. He was a Grand Wizard of the Ku Klux Klan and a member of the American Nazi Party. I have been hearing about his vile activities for many years. I only saw the funny side of this when my son Grant said to me, 'I wonder if he gets lots of enquiries about *Tell Me on a Sunday*.'

DIAMONDS ARE FOREVER

Too many people cling to the grief that comes from failure and not enough cling to the thrill that comes from success.

Oscar Hammerstein

L uck plays a big part in the life of every songwriter. We live from disappointment to disappointment. I can't tell you how many times my publisher has called me to say that it looks like I've got the next Celine Dion single, or British Airways is thinking of using 'Born Free' for their new television commercial. I thought I was heading for another disappointment when John Barry and I met with one of the James Bond producers, Harry Saltzman, to play him our song. As soon as he heard it, Harry said, 'I don't like the tune and the words are filthy!' John's short fuse kicked in and he said, 'Well, what the fuck do you know about songs?' Harry got up, his face slowly turning crimson, and walked out, slamming the door. Thankfully, the other Bond producer, Cubby Broccoli, loved it and so did Shirley Bassey. It was touch and go for a while and I was relieved when it ended up in the picture.

Writing songs is the best part of any assignment. Playing the finished work to producers and directors can be an uphill climb. Anyone can criticise a lyric but they can't criticise music. I've never heard a producer say to a composer, 'I don't like the modulation in bar 47.' I learned early on that songs have to sing. What I mean by that is lyrics, as opposed to poems, are written to be sung.

The great Sammy Cahn used to talk a lot about what he called 'singability'. He said, 'Songs have to sing effortlessly, and words will not sing unless properly wedded to the proper notes and the words have to have air around them to make them crystal clear.' He gave a rather extreme example of clunky lyric-writing. He said, 'Try singing "Love can laugh at locksmiths".' Funny man, Sammy.

'Diamonds Are Forever' turned out to be too long for the opening titles so we had to cut a verse. I've included the lyric to the discarded verse below.

At the recording session Shirley didn't know how to approach the song. John Barry said, 'You have to think of a diamond as a penis.' We all laughed at this, but that was a very useful note because after that she sang the song with great conviction.

> Diamonds are forever,
> They are all I need to please me,
> They can stimulate and tease me,
> They won't leave in the night,
> I've no fear that they might desert me.
>
> Diamonds are forever,
> Hold one up and then caress it,
> Touch it, stroke it, and undress it,
> I can see every part,
> Nothing hides in the heart to hurt me.
>
> I don't need love,
> For what good would love do me?
> Diamonds never lie to me,

DIAMONDS ARE FOREVER

For when love's gone,
They'll lustre on.

Diamonds are forever
Sparkling round my little finger
Unlike men the diamonds linger
Men are mere mortals who
Are not worth going to your grave for

[discarded verse]
Diamonds are forever
I can taste the satisfaction
Flawless physical attraction
Bitter cold, icy fresh
Till they rest on the flesh
They crave for

Diamonds are forever, forever, forever,
Diamonds are forever, forever, forever,
Forever, and ever.

SNOOKER

How beautiful to do nothing and then rest afterwards.

Spanish proverb

My father used to play snooker in a local hall in Hackney and he would often take me with him. As a result I became hooked on the game, and I attribute my sanity to that green-baize haven. I became a member of the RAC Club in Pall Mall, and when I play the game I can think of nothing else apart from potting and positioning balls. I must say that I'm not very good at the game, just an enthusiast. I love the mixture of elegance and treachery and the sounds of clicking balls; the reds, the yellow, green, brown, blue, pink and the much sought-after black. It's a sort of quiet excitement. If anyone gets a break over fifteen we ask them to take a urine test. We each copy those phrases that the snooker commentators use on television: 'He's still got a bit of work to do' or 'This could be a clearance'. Sometimes I look at my watch and I can't believe I've been playing for two hours. A game of snooker and a sandwich. That's not much for a man to ask, is it?

Whenever I go to New York I make sure I spend some time at the New York Athletic Club. They have a brilliant billiard room and it has helped clear my head many times when working on troubled musicals.

Mozart was a frequent billiard player, as were Ira Gershwin, Babe Ruth and Mark Twain. Mark Twain was so enamoured of the game he wrote a poem about it:

'Cushion First'

When all your days are dark with doubt
And dying hope is at its worst:
When all life's balls are scattered wide,
With not a shot in sight, to left or right,
Don't give it up:
Advance your cue and shut your eyes,
And take the cushion first.

Most people in showbusiness play golf, but I much prefer snooker. I can honestly say that not once in forty years of playing snooker have I ever lost a ball.

I played with the great composer Marvin Hamlisch and it was hilarious. I thought he was dreadful at the game until I figured out that he was colour blind!

JIM STEINMAN

While John Barry ate very little, another collaborator of mine ate everything. Jim Steinman is the genius producer and writer of *Bat Out of Hell*. He was over here writing a musical version of *Whistle Down the Wind* with Andrew. He stayed at the Dorchester and had this expensive habit of ordering many dishes for his main meal. Waiters would bring up trolleys with pasta, chicken, lamb, beef and fish.

I wrote a couple of songs with him and he was a delight to work with. One song of ours was 'Is Nothing Sacred', which was recorded by Celine Dion and Meatloaf. Jim's a fabulous character and a total original, and this quote by the legendary beat poet Jack Kerouac sort of sums him up: 'The people that interest me are the gloriously mad ones. The ones who are mad to live . . . mad to sing. The ones who never yawn or say a commonplace thing. The ones who burn burn burn like famous Roman candles exploding like spiders across the stars.'

THE MAN WITH THE GOLDEN GUN

This was my third James Bond song and it reunited me with the fabulous Lulu. We had such great success earlier with 'To Sir, With Love' and we were so excited about this new adventure. Unfortunately it came at a time when John Barry was busier than he'd ever been. He was up to his eyes with John Schlesinger's film *The Day of the Locust* when he was asked to do *Golden Gun*. He wrote the melody quickly, which wasn't like John. He usually liked to live with a song before he was ready to unveil it to the world. It wasn't a difficult lyric to write because the requirement was so specific. It was about a great assassin who killed with a golden gun. On reflection, I think we should have used the title in the middle of the song the way Carole Bayer Sager did with 'The Spy Who Loved Me'. I tried to make the lyric a delicious piece of nonsense – a piece of cartoon hokum. Lulu enjoyed the experience but thought the song should have been sung by Shirley Bassey as it needed her kind of vocal power. *The Hollywood Reporter* gave us a good review: 'John Barry keeps his James Bond theme music fresh and adventuresome, with amusing lyrics by Don Black.'

> He has a powerful weapon
> He charges a million a shot

THE SANEST GUY IN THE ROOM

An assassin that's second to none

The man with the golden gun

Lurking in some darkened doorway

Or crouched on a rooftop somewhere

In the next room or this very one

The man with the golden gun

Love is required

Whenever he's hired

It comes just before the kill

No man can catch him

No hit man can match him

For his million-dollar skill

One golden shot means another poor victim

Has come to a glittering end

For a price he'll erase anyone

The man with the golden gun

His eye may be

On you or me

Who will he bang?

We shall see

One golden shot means another poor victim

Has come to a glittering end

If you want to get rid of someone

The man with the golden gun

Will get it done

He'll shoot anyone

With his golden gun.

NOTHING IN THE WORLD WILL EVER BE THE SAME

Love turns the smallest gesture into an event.

Arnold Wesker, playwright

It has been twelve months since Shirley died and I still feel a sense of disbelief about it. I had dinner last year with David Walliams who said that I must be the luckiest man in the world to have lived happily with the same woman for sixty years. He added, 'That could never happen again in today's world.' I was in a taxi recently and I told the young Afghan driver about my loss and he spoke such unexpected words of wisdom. 'Your wife spent her whole life loving you and making you happy and she'd be very upset with you if you didn't live your life to the full.'

So many people say comforting words, and although their words make sense, there is only a brief comfort in them. We shared a lifetime of unrivalled happiness. Since I've been on my own, nearly everyone I've met has had a troubled marriage, which makes me feel ours was unique. It seems most couples have their ups and downs, but I feel like we never had any downs. The pain of what has happened is still raw, and yet it's a pain I don't want to heal. The rawness of it brings her closer.

I console myself in knowing that she is now at peace and I made her very happy. I also know I made her laugh a lot. As an old stand-up comedian you have no idea what it's like to have an appreciative audience day and night.

Shirley was never impressed with megastars or glitzy opening nights. The family was everything to her. And yet, when she did attend an opening night, in my eyes she was the most beautiful and stylish person there. Maureen Lipman once said that Shirley was the salt of the earth in a glamorous shaker. She was also summed up beautifully by the journalist John Nathan who said: 'Shirley is a good-looking woman who has the elegance of someone accustomed to expensive things but the no-nonsense manner of someone who doesn't care much about them.'

No one was more generous than her. Whenever I said, 'Let's go on a cruise,' or 'Don't you think it's time we changed the car?' she would say 'I'd rather give the money to the boys. I want to see them happy and settled while I'm still here.' I count myself very lucky that I still have a very small interest in my house.

Shirley was also very quick-witted and always made me laugh. On her eightieth birthday she began her speech like this:

'I've been very lucky in the life that I've led. I have met some incredibly starry people over the years, but I'm delighted to say that none of them are here tonight!'

Bill Kenwright the producer said that he always thought The Everly Brothers were the greatest ever duo until he met me and Shirley.

I was trying to think of something she did to annoy me and all I could come up with was this: when she did the *Daily Mail* quick crossword she would write the answer to one across in ink before checking if it tallied with one down. No matter what success I had I always thought she could have done better than me.

Shirley could mix with anyone. Although she came from a council flat in Clapton she could make friends with people whose children were called Crispin or Rupert or Tarquin.

A couple of years ago she had breast cancer. That came as a shock but the bigger shock was that she even bothered to mention it. Shirley was the sort of woman you read or hear about but never actually meet. The perfect wife, mother, daughter, sister and friend. She was the rock who made sure that me and our boys would sail, climb, soar. If she had one fault it's that she never prepared us for something like this. But then nothing could.

It's a Jewish tradition that within a year of a person passing there should be what we call a stone setting. This is where family and friends gather to reflect and see the memorial stone. Shirley is buried at the Edgwarebury Lane cemetery. Her epitaph reads: No One Will Ever Be More Missed.

Over the years, whenever I had to make a speech I would run it by Shirley first. She was brilliant at spotting any kind of false note. She used to say to me just be yourself, don't try to be clever, just be honest and speak from your heart. I had to say a few words again, but without her checking them first. These were the ones I chose:

'Today I was going to quote my favourite lines from the W. H. Auden poem "Stop All the Clocks":

> You were my North, my South, my East and West
> My working week and my Sunday rest
> My noon, my midnight, my talk, my song
> I thought love would last forever. I was wrong.'

But I could hear Shirley saying clearly, "That's very lovely but it all sounds a bit hi falutin to me." Then I was going to quote that marvellous line from Don McLean's song "Vincent" – "This world was never meant for one as beautiful as you." But again, I could hear Shirley's voice saying "It sounds too considered, too written, too prepared. What you say should come across as spontaneous and most of all truthful." So I came up with:

'When I met Shirley more than sixty years ago not only was she beautiful but she read books and cried at sad songs. I knew then that she would be the love of my life for the rest of my life.'

I can now hear Shirley saying – That's fine, go with that.

For every birthday and anniversary since the day we met I would write her a poem. She always looked forward to opening her card, and it always seemed to bring on a tear and a smile. This was the last one I wrote, for her eightieth birthday.

I never bought a card with eighty on it
With an old woman in lace gloves
And a lilac bonnet
That wouldn't be right
That wouldn't be true
That kind of eighty
Just isn't you
In my eyes you're as ageless
As you were at seventeen
Your skin is still as flawless
And your eyes are still as green
In my eyes you're still the princess
That always took my breath away
In my eyes you're still the song
My heart sings night and day

In my eyes there's no one
In this world like you
But don't forget I'm short-sighted
And I've got glaucoma too.'

Coping with the loss is truly beyond words. The last line of
the song 'Love Changes Everything' comes close: 'Nothing in the
world will ever be the same.'

DOWNTON ABBEY AND EASTENDERS

In the same article where Mark Steyn called me the sanest guy in the room, he also said, 'Living in London Don has to go from writing Broadway shows with Jule Styne to naff assignments like putting words to television themes.' I don't see it that way. I think all assignments present a lyrical challenge and I enjoy all of them whether it's a Bond song, a pop song, a movie song or a TV commercial for Pepsi Cola. I have the same routine for all of them: a walk in the park or endless teas in the kitchen.

Downton Abbey was the biggest series on television not only here but globally. I had a call from the composer John Lunn one day and he asked me if I would put words to the main theme. I had never seen the show or heard the main theme but John came to my house, played it to me and I instantly fell in love with the melody. He also showed me a two- or three-minute scene where two people were saying goodbye at a railway station. It reminded me a little bit of *Brief Encounter*. The young man in the scene was going off to war and the sad-eyed girl looked heartbroken. That was all I had to go on, so I wrote a lyric from the girl's point of view and called the song 'Did I Make the Most of Loving You?' It is sung beautifully on the *Downton Abbey* album by singer Mary-Jess. There is now talk of a musical based on the series and the film.

Did I make the most of loving you?
So many things we didn't do
Did I give you all my heart could give?
Two unlived lives with lives to live
When these endless lonely nights are through
I'll make the most of loving you
I'll make the most of loving you

Did we make the most of what we had?
Not seeing you makes my heart sad
Did we make the most of summer days?
We still have time to change our ways
When these endless lonely days are through
I'll make the most of loving you
I'll make the most of loving you
I'll make the most of loving you

Did those tender words stay in my head?
So many things were left unsaid
Did I give you all my heart could give
Two unlived lives with lives to live

When these endless lonely days are through
I'll make the most of loving you
I'll make the most of loving you
I'll make the most of loving you

The *Eastenders* theme is probably the most well known of all television themes in the UK. It was written by Simon May, who also wrote the haunting theme to *Howard's Way*. I subsequently put words to that and called it 'Always There' – it was recorded by Marti Webb. Again, I had never really seen an episode of Eastenders but when I was asked to write a lyric I made a point of watching a few. It struck me that a lot of people were having affairs, mostly troubled ones. I came up with the title 'Anyone Can Fall in Love' and it was recorded by Anita Dobson who played the part of Angie in the series. Her record went to number two in the hit parade.

> Anyone can fall in love
> That's the easy part you must keep it going
> Anyone can fall in love
> Over the years it has to keep growing
> Sun and rain
> Joy and pain
> There's highs – there's lows
> We've no way of knowing.
>
> Anyone can fall in love
> That's not hard to do it isn't so clever
> Anyone can fall in love
> But you must make the love last forever . . .
> Who can say
> Love will stay?
> It's up to you
> Don't hide what needs showing.
>
> Anyone can fall in love
> That's the easy part you must keep it going

DOWNTON ABBEY AND EASTENDERS

Everyone can fall in love
But you must make the love last forever more
How do you keep the music from dying?
Love falls asleep unless you keep trying

Anyone can fall in love
Life's more than that, it's pulling together
Everyone can share the love
Where we come from friends never say never
Side by side
Satisfied
To stay right here in one square forever.

Anyone can fall in love
That's not hard to do it isn't so clever
Anyone can fall in love
But you must make the love last forever more

▌WHERE WERE YOU SITTING?

One of the most difficult things to achieve in the theatre is the sound balance between the orchestra and the singer. It is frustrating for the audience but to a lyric writer it's a nightmare. Every show I've been involved with has ended up with me saying to the sound man, 'I can't hear all the lyrics.' I always get the same answer, 'Where were you sitting?' This doesn't only apply to my shows, it happens so many times in musicals. I cannot enjoy the show if I can't hear what they're singing about. I've seen the musical *Chess* many times and never enjoyed it completely because I couldn't follow the story. The songs are great but you can't follow the plot if you can't hear the words. It's only when I saw the show at the London Coliseum that I enjoyed it all because the lyrics were on a screen, as often is the case in the world of opera. I discussed this at length with the show's lyric writer Tim Rice. He agreed with me and said he cringes every time the words are inaudible especially in choral numbers.

In musicals the lyrics tell the story and must be heard. In the world of opera the music is the most important element. You can see a wonderful opera and not understand a single word, those beautiful melodies and just a rough idea of the plot will be more than enough to send you home happy, elated or moved to tears depending largely on the music.

And why is it that I can hear what pop singers are saying on the *X Factor* when they talk about the inspiration for the song they are about to sing – it's always a heartbreaking tale about loss and deep despair and they can barely hold themselves together when telling us about the emotions that led them to write the song. But when they start singing you can't hear a bloody word! At least when this happens you're only pulling your hair out for about three minutes, but in a musical it's a long and garbled evening. I once had a T-shirt made with the words Where Were You Sitting? on it. I have never ever found the perfect place to sit in a theatre to hear all the words in all the songs. I can't believe I'm the only one.

BAR MITZVAH BOY

In a musical nothing is all right until it's too late to be changed. **Jack Rosenthal**

O n the surface, Jule Styne was the role model for every movie actor who played a Broadway composer. He was short, nervy, dynamic. He smoked a lot, was an addicted gambler, threw the odd temper tantrum, and oh, I almost forgot, he wrote some of the best songs ever written for the stage and cinema. Every time I went to New York I would see him in his office above the Mark Hellinger theatre. Up those fire-escape-type stairs into a smoky, legendary slice of musical history. Here was Jule to the manor born: motioning you to help yourself to coffee while he was on the phone to his bookmaker. He liked to bet on every race. Sometimes these were just a five-dollar bet, no big deal, but from the look on his face you'd think he had the family heirlooms riding on it. His office was a modest one, cluttered with copies of *Variety*, scripts and manuscript paper and an old upright piano. Nothing flash and he liked it this way. He believed the best songs were written over a corned-beef sandwich in a cold rehearsal room or a smoke-filled bedroom at two in the morning. He told me that he wanted to work with Alan Jay Lerner but he knew it wouldn't work out when Alan drew up to his office in a Rolls Royce.

Jule had a sentimental side too. He must have told me this story about his mother a dozen times, but he enjoyed telling it so much I didn't have the heart to stop him. His mother lived in Chicago and four nights a week she would go to the Yiddish Theatre. One day Jule called her and said he would be in Chicago and he asked her to think of somewhere special they could go together. Without hesitation she said 'the Yiddish Theatre'. Jule said, 'But Ma, you go there all the time.' She answered, 'But not with you.' Every time he told this story he had to fight hard to stop the tears from coming.

To sit and write songs with him was great fun. The problem with working with a legend is that you have to be diplomatic if there's something you don't like about a melody, especially when before he plays it he pulls you closer to him and whispers, 'This may just be the best motherfucking tune I've ever come up with!' That's some statement when you consider he came up with 'Time After Time', 'It's Magic', 'Three Coins in the Fountain', 'Everything's Coming Up Roses', 'People', 'Diamonds Are a Girl's Best Friend' and about 1400 more.

What a roller-coaster ride *Bar Mitzvah Boy* was. The director was the hottest guy on Broadway, Martin Charnin, who had just written the lyrics to and directed the monster hit musical *Annie*. The book writer was our very own brilliant Jack Rosenthal. I couldn't have been more excited. It all started off so brilliantly, we all loved each other and each other's work.

It's hard to believe that Jule was born in Bethnal Green in London. I remember driving round this rather drab part of town. I also showed him where I was born in Hackney, just a mile or so away. He said that when you come from these sorts of beginnings it helps you to understand the feelings and dreams of ordinary people. One could pick holes in this theory as there have been a lot of brilliant songwriters who happened to be born wealthy. But when Jule had a theory, you looked at his dreamy Peter Pan expression and kind of went along with it.

Jack Rosenthal seemed like the odd man out in the creative quartet. I was in awe of Jule's talent and I thought Martin Charnin did a fabulous job with *Annie*. Jack was never really a musicals kind of guy and often looked baffled at the three of us getting overexcited by very little. We were all thrilled with Jack's book for the show and Jule kept telling him what a genius he was. That is until we did a first preview which didn't go down too well. All of a sudden we saw a different side to affable Jule. He screamed at Jack, 'When are we gonna get some flesh on these cardboard fuckin' characters??' As with most musicals, rewrite followed rewrite. I think the basic problem with the show was that it was about a very ordinary Jewish family from suburban Willesden and Martin Charnin brought a Broadway sheen to it that was out of place. Also, the orchestrations were polished and glitzy. We have since had smaller productions that work much better than the original over-produced one. Although the show wasn't a success it kind of changed my life. I received two telegrams after the opening night; one from director Michael Bennett (*A Chorus Line*) which read, 'Best lyrics I've ever heard on a West End stage'; and another one from director Hal Prince (*West Side Story*) which read, 'Impeccable work, bravo.' These telegrams took all the sting out of the bad reviews. A few days later I got a call from Andrew Lloyd Webber. He wondered if we could write something together, and the lunch we had after that call turned out to be life-changing as it led to our first collaboration, *Tell Me on a Sunday*. I have since written many more songs with him than Tim Rice. has

Bar Mitzvah Boy tells the story of thirteen-year-old Eliot Green who is about to have his bar mitzvah. His neurotic mother Rita is having a very Jewish breakdown worrying herself ill about the upcoming function. Her main worries, apart from her hair, are the seating plan and how many will be there. She sits down with a pen and paper, makes a list, and sings 'The Cohens Are Coming':

> The Cohens are coming
> The Friedmans are coming
> The Schneiders the Spiros
> The Katzs and Shapiros
> The Kleins are coming
> The Solomans are coming
> The Feingolds, the Shermans
> The Levys and the Bermans
> The Mendels are coming
> The Rubins are coming
> And the Schwartzs, the Newmans
> The Roses and the Schumans
> The Glicks are coming
> Rabinowitz is coming
> The Barnets, the Hymans
> The Silvers and the Simons
> The Segals are coming
> The Goodmans are coming
> The Myers, the Gellers
> The Fishmans and the Sellars
> The Blooms are coming
> The Lawrences are coming

THE SANEST GUY IN THE ROOM

The Suzmans, the Costers
The Franklyns and the Posters

Now counting up this list of names
And adding Joe and Woolfy James
Plus Cyril Moss and Josephine
And Monty Gold and Geraldine
Lionel Marks and his Pauline
Jennifer and Lou Levine
Including Harold, and Grandad and Leslie
Eliot and Rita and Victor Green
It makes a grand total of
One hundred and seventeen!

Bar mitzvahs come
Bar mitzvahs go
But there's not one
Like the one we're gonna throw
Whoever comes will know they've been
To the bar mitzvah of Eliot
Mazeltov Eliot
Bar mitzvah of Eliot Green

JULE STYNE AND SAMMY CAHN

One of Jule Styne's first big hits was 'I Don't Want to Walk Without You, Baby', which he wrote with Frank Loesser. They loved writing together but Frank was called up and had to go in the army. So Jule had to find another lyric writer. Frank's advice to him was to find someone who could write warm and clever lyrics, not someone who was fixated on rhymes. He said there is such a thing as a rhyming dictionary and you can find a rhyme for anything. So, Jule was recommended to try working with a hungry and ambitious lyricist by the name of Sammy Cahn. It turned out to be one of the greatest songwriting partnerships of all time.

Jule Styne told me this story of when he and Sammy Cahn started out. It was a Saturday night and Sammy had a little black book filled with girls' names he would like to date. He couldn't reach any of them so he ended up without a date. He stayed home and wrote a lyric. Next day he handed the lyric to Jule Styne and within a couple of days Frank Sinatra recorded it. The song was called 'Saturday Night Is the Loneliest Night of the Week'. It turned out to be one of their biggest hits.

I remember speaking with Sammy Cahn about his amazing list of hits and was surprised when he asked me to guess which one of them made the most money. I had a stab at 'Come Fly with Me' and 'Let it Snow' or 'It's Magic'. I could have gone on and on but he interrupted me to say it was 'Three Coins in the Fountain'. The reason for this is that it had to be written so quickly there was no time to do a publishing deal. Apparently the producer Sol Siegel walked into Jule Styne's and Sammy's office and said, 'Can you guys write a song called "Three Coins in the Fountain" for my new movie?' Sammy said, 'Sure, can we see a script?' The producer replied, 'There's no time for that, we need it right away.' Sammy said, 'Can we see the film?' The reply came, 'No time for that either, there's bits of it all over the lot.' Sammy said, 'Well what's it about?' Mr Siegel said, 'Three girls go to Rome hoping to find love and they throw coins in the fountain.' 'That's enough,' said Sammy. They wrote the song that day, Frank Sinatra recorded it right away, it became a massive hit and won an Oscar for Best Song in a Motion Picture. Only then did the studio realise they never made a deal for the song. Sammy and Jule ended up with half the publishing rights, making this their biggest money-earner.

One of the best nights I ever had in the theatre was watching Sammy Cahn in his one-man show. He sang his songs badly but with feeling, and he had so many anecdotes about Hollywood, Frank Sinatra and all the people he met. I remember his funny story about when he met the Hungarian classical composer Nicholas Brodszky and he was asked to put a lyric to his melody for an Italian singer. Sammy said Mr Brodszky played the piano as if he had eleven fingers on each hand! It was so flowery and busy. When he finished playing the composer said to Sammy, 'Can you put a lyric to that?' Sammy said, 'I could if I could hear the tune'. Eventually Mr Brodszky played the melody with one finger and Sammy put some words to it. Oh, the Italian singer turned out to be Mario Lanza and the song was 'Be My Love'.

CAPPED TEETH AND CAESAR SALAD

Hollywood is a place where they put you under contract instead of under observation. **Kenneth Tynan**

There was also an opportunity in *Tell Me on a Sunday* to poke fun at the Hollywood lifestyle through a song called 'Capped Teeth and Caesar Salad'. My many trips to L.A. helped me write it. I can't tell you how many times I've rewritten this song because every time there was a new production Andrew and I felt it should be updated with the changing culture over there. Here's the last rewrite I did:

> Capped Teeth and Caesar Salad
> Healthy Beverly Hills
> No booze and no red meat
> You have to stay petite
> You're allowed to bonk
> But no red plonk
> Out here everyone's la la
> That's why it's called L.A.
> Go wild once in a while
> With a large camomile
> I'll email you and
> Have a nice day

CAPPED TEETH AND CAESAR SALAD

Botox, Ashtanga yoga
Starstruck Beverly Hills
Where every woman shops
'Til her chauffeur drops
When her bosoms droop
Fifty surgeons swoop
'Waiter, she'll take the yoghurt
And a cold Perrier'
She's eaten nothing fried
Since the old Queen died
Let's stay in touch and
Have a nice day

Capped teeth and Caesar salad
Unreal Beverly Hills
An eighty-year-old man
Behaves like Peter Pan
Wears a baseball cap
Buys his clothes from Gap
No one's left in the closet
No big deal to be gay
Both men and women go
In search of Russell Crowe
I'll have to run now
Have a nice day
I'll call you back and
Have a nice day

TELL ME ON A SUNDAY

I first met Andrew at the Society of Distinguished Songwriters meeting. Andrew never really fitted into a lads' night out setting. He felt awkward at the sort of childish aimlessness of it all, which was exactly what appealed to the other members. These members included Justin ('Knights in White Satin') Hayward, Tony ('Love Grows Where My Rosemary Goes') Macaulay, Graham (I'm Not In Love) Gouldman, etc.

There seemed to be an instant bond between us as I was the only member there who had written a couple of musicals, *Billy* and *Bar Mitzvah Boy*. Andrew was particularly impressed that I wrote with Jule Styne, who had written *Gypsy* and *Funny Girl*. I got a call from him one day and he asked me to lunch at Ma Maison in Knightsbridge. He had already written *Superstar*, *Joseph*, and more recently, *Evita*. We talked about doing a simple one-woman show and we got talking about how fashionable it was for English girls to go to America to try and 'find themselves'. We thought we could build a story around that flimsy premise. After lunch we walked to my flat in Basil Street where Andrew played me a tune he'd just written. Within twenty-four hours I came up with the words and called it 'Come Back with the Same Look in Your Eyes'. I imagined that our lone girl would be saying goodbye to her lover at some point in the show and the song would fit that kind of narrative. That's how it all began and it was a wonderful and thrilling collaboration. He was living in Eaton Place which was just a walk from my flat in Basil Street and we used to meet often to concoct the storyline. I would come with lyrical thoughts and song titles and Andrew was never stuck in coming up with the right tune. He is also not married to every note he writes. The lyric of the song 'Tell Me on a Sunday' didn't quite fit his melody so he altered it. He is flexible and open-minded, which may surprise some people. He is also very aware of his reputation for being difficult, and I think from time to time he enjoys it. When we were about to present *Sunset Boulevard* at his Sydmonton home, he looked at his watch, which said 11.45. We were due to start at noon. He leaned over to me and said, 'I think I have time for one more tantrum.'

I suppose the breakthrough arrived when we came up with the idea of our girl falling in love with a phoney Hollywood producer called Sheldon Bloom. It gave us the chance to come up with a comedy song about Hollywood called 'Capped Teeth and Caesar Salad'. Also, one day Andrew called me and said, 'What about if she writes letters home to her mother?' This was a great idea and we used to write many of these letters over the phone. Of course it helps if you know who you are writing for, so we had to come up with the right actress. She had to have a great voice, be in her late twenties and be very down to earth, as we imagined she was an ordinary girl from Muswell Hill. We were remarkably lucky to come up with Marti Webb.

The project was very successful. We had a huge single hit with 'Take That Look Off Your Face', the album was a big seller and it was filmed for the BBC and repeated within six weeks. I believe that was a first for a musical show. It was also critically acclaimed and I remember one newspaper, alluding to Andrew's fractious relationship with Tim Rice, saying Andrew had lost his Larry Hart but found his Hammerstein.

As nearly every song was about a girl's emotions, I had loads of letters saying how do you know so much about women's feelings, especially as you've been married to the same woman for years. It's a question I still get asked. Again, I don't really know but I have always loved the way women think and I've always been fascinated by the power, the intensity and madness of love. The producer Bill Kenwright once wrote to me and said, 'You have had what appears to be the best and most stable relationship of any man I have known yet your emotional observations always get me right in the solar plexus!'

The first time I went to Andrew's Sydmonton house was probably the coldest and murkiest day of the year. Shirley and I didn't think we'd ever get there. When we did arrive Andrew greeted us wearing a short-sleeved summery shirt. That was the first time I realised that he was different to other men. He isn't just interested in diverse subjects like musicals, architecture, art, finance, cats and botany, he is absolutely besotted. When I feel I've come up with the right lyric there is definitely an inner glow inside me. When Andrew finds the right tune the elation is palpable. Try and imagine an anthropologist who has unearthed a lost kingdom. I must own up to pretending I know what he's talking about when it comes to key signatures and 5/4 bars and 7/8 bars but it all goes over my head. Yet I can see it's all desperately important to him. Somehow or other I can write words to very complicated music but when he says, 'What do you think of that 6/8 section?' I have to resort to, 'Will you la la that bit to me?'

The first time Andrew came to my flat I warned him that he would see something he hasn't seen for years. He said, 'What's that?' I said, 'Blank walls.' I have been friends with all of his three wives, Sarah Norris, Sarah Brightman and Madeleine Gurdon. I was very proud when twenty-three years ago Madeleine and Andrew asked me to be a godfather to their newly born son Alastair. I made a speech about it at Alastair's twenty-first birthday party which was received with great laughter:

> I have been researching what the obligations of a godfather are and they are quite strict, funnily enough, but not if you are a Jewish godfather. You are supposed to bring him up to be a regular churchgoer, but as far as I'm concerned I have no strong feelings about this. You are also obliged, in the event he suffers financial insecurity, to somehow shield him in difficult times. In twenty-one years I have never wavered from that risky responsibility.

Andrew's enthusiasm is so stimulating and I also love the way he doesn't squander words. He gets straight to the point. One thing that used to unsettle me was the way he asks people's opinions of a song he's just written. When you're creating a song it's easy to be influenced by someone in the office not liking it. This same thing used to happen to Irving Berlin. Mr. Berlin's secretary didn't think much of 'How Deep Is the Ocean' and Richard Rodgers wasn't bowled over with 'There's No Business

Like Show Business'. The two songs stayed in his trunk for many years before they saw the light of day. I'm not sure John Barry was wrong when he said, 'A little arrogance from a writer is not such a bad thing.'

'Tell Me on a Sunday'

Don't write a letter when you want to leave
Don't call me at three a.m. from a friend's apartment
I'd like to choose how I hear the news
Take me to a park that's covered with trees
Tell me on a Sunday please
Let me down easy, no big song and dance
No long faces, no long looks
No deep conversation
I know the way we should spend that day
Take me to a zoo that's got chimpanzees
Tell me on a Sunday please

Don't want to know who's to blame
It won't help knowing
Don't want to fight day and night
Bad enough you're going

Don't leave in silence, with no word at all
Don't get drunk and slam the door
That's no way to end this
I know how I want you to say goodbye
Find a circus ring with a flying trapeze

Tell me on a Sunday please . . .
Don't run off in the pouring rain,
Don't call me as they call your plane,
Take the hurt out of all the pain

Take me to a park that's covered with trees
Tell me on a Sunday please

The big song from *Tell Me on a Sunday* turned out to be a surprise. We had recorded all but one of the songs – one I originally called 'You Must Be Mistaken'. Marti Webb's vocal was so fabulous that the three of us looked at each other feeling we'd left the best till last. The record company agreed and, after hearing the record a dozen times or more, I changed the title to 'Take That Look Off Your Face'.

You must be mistaken
It couldn't have been
You couldn't have seen him yesterday
He's doing some deal up in Baltimore now
I hate it when he's away
You must be mistaken
I'm sure that you are
There's more than one car with stickers on
And lots of young guys wear corduroy pants
And I'd know if he hadn't gone

Take that look off your face
I can see through your smile

131

You would love to be right

I bet you didn't sleep good last night

Couldn't wait to bring all of that bad news to my door

Well I've got news for you

I knew before

If I'm not mistaken

It started last year

I'm not very clear when it began

I noticed a change but I just closed my eyes

As only a woman can

No I didn't dig deep

I did not want to know

Well you don't interfere

When you're scared of the things you might hear

When he's back you think

 I will end it right there and then

Well my fair-weather friend

You're wrong again

Take that look off your face

I can see through your smile

You would love to be right

I bet you didn't sleep good last night

Couldn't wait to bring all of that bad news to my door

Well I've got news for you

I knew before

TELL ME ON A SUNDAY – MALE VERSION

It's probably around ten years ago that people started suggesting a gay version of *Tell Me on a Sunday*. I always thought that it could work but did nothing to further it along. Then one day I got a letter from Richard Maltby, the American director of the New York production of *Song and Dance*. He told me that a friend of his had put together a version in a rehearsal room for a few friends to see if the idea would work. Richard was there and said it played better than the straight version. I have great respect for Richard so I recently spent a few days on this in London with the actor and singer Jonathan Bailey and the director Rebecca Frecknall. It was surprisingly powerful and touching. We made very few changes to the original, although I'm sure more will be coming if this moves ahead. As the piece is set in the Eighties I wanted to make a reference to the Aids epidemic. I did this in a letter our man writes home to his mother:

> Mum, I know you read the papers
> Don't you worry I'll be careful
> They say that every hour
> Another gay man dies
> And yes we're climbing walls
> Since we heard about Rock Hudson

133

THE SANEST GUY IN THE ROOM

The news has taken everyone
In Key West by surprise!

A new song, 'Dreams Never Run On Time', will be featured, towards the end of the show after his string of disastrous relationships. In his letter to his mum he writes:

I won't be down for long mum
It isn't in my make up
Bouncing back's one of the gifts
I got from dad and you . . .

'Dreams Never Run On Time'

I don't want to hear
Any more sad songs
About broken hearts
When it comes to love
I have learned you must
Roll with the punches
Something good will come
Out of all of this
No doubt in my mind
If it's up to me
Then I'll be just fine
I'm a believer
Living without love
Is not a crime
Like a slow night train

That's caught in the rain

Dreams never run on time

I won't tie myself

In all kinds of knots

Like I've done before

I remember when

I could laugh at life

I'm still that person

I won't count the days

I won't fall apart

That's not who I am

I know dreams will start

When they're meant to start

I'm in no hurry

Reaching for rainbows

Is quite a climb

I'll ride them again

I can't tell you when

Dreams never run on time

I won't tie myself

In all kinds of knots

Like I've done before

I remember when

I could laugh at life

I'm still that person

I won't count the days

I won't fall apart

That's not who I am

135

THE SANEST GUY IN THE ROOM

I know dreams will start

When they're meant to start

I'm in no hurry

Reaching for rainbows

Is quite a climb

Sometimes you're afraid

But you're only delayed

Dreams never run on time

WHEN YOU LEAST EXPECT IT

I have written over two thousand songs that between them cover almost every human emotion. Without doubt the hardest thing to put into words are the emotions that come with grief. What makes it difficult, or almost impossible, is to write about it without sounding mawkish. I come across everyday notes in Shirley's handwriting that say 'must buy bananas' or 'call dentist' and there is no way in the world that I can throw them away. Her hairbrush, her Vaseline lip salve, her dressing gown, they have all become priceless treasures. If you've never known grief this probably sounds daft, but if you've loved someone deeply for a very long time it will make complete sense.

A little while ago on a sunny morning I went for a stroll to the Westfield shopping centre to buy a pair of trainers. I decided to stop for lunch and when I saw the menu a vivid memory engulfed and unsettled me. I hadn't realised that I haven't had a baked potato for two years. This was one of Shirley's favourite simple meals. I could hear her saying, 'You can eat the skin, I've washed it.' A baked potato, a flower stall, a stylish scarf. Even these emotions have been captured in a song by lyricist Hal David – 'There's Always Something There To Remind Me'.

A friend of mine, the American songwriter Paul Williams, wrote a line in a song that comes the closest I've ever come across to the stark reality of loss. It's from his song 'You and Me Against the World'. It's the last line that says it all:

> And when one of us is gone
> And one of us is left alone to carry on
> Then remembering will have to do.
> No matter how many times you tell yourself how lucky you have
> been and what a wonderful life you shared, from here on in
> 'remembering will have to do'.

TRUE GRIT AND MERLIN

I loved spending time with Elmer Bernstein, who was recognised as one of the greatest movie composers of all time. He had graphic stories about the early days of Hollywood. His big moment came when Cecil B. DeMille was shooting *The Ten Commandments* and Elmer was asked to audition for him. He had been rehearsing the theme he had written for days. Finally, he found himself sitting at the piano, straight-backed as in the typical concert pianist position. He played his theme in the most dramatic, theatrical and overwrought way in order to sell it to the great man. When he finished Mr. DeMille said, 'Can you now play it with one finger?' He got the job and many others including *To Kill a Mockingbird, The Magnificent Seven, Birdman of Alcatraz* and dozens of other landmark scores.

Over the years I wrote eight movie songs and one Broadway musical with Elmer. The films are mostly forgotten apart from a couple of John Wayne films, *Cahill US Marshall* and *True Grit*.

True Grit was a lousy title for a song, but in those days a song in a picture was inclined to be given the same title as the film. It's great publicity for the film if the song is being played on radios around the world. I remember when Elmer and I had a meeting with the great John Wayne, who was also the producer of the film. He had enormous hands and spoke the way that impressionists mimicked him. I asked him if he had any ideas for the song we were about to write and he said, 'Do what the hell you like as long as you call it "True Grit".' I'd written some movie songs with bad titles before: 'The House of a Thousand Dolls', 'Mr. Jericho' and 'The Midas Run' to name just a few. I always envied those writers who were given titles like 'The Way We Were' or 'Love Is a Many Splendored Thing'. The luck of the draw, I guess. Although when the song got nominated for an Academy Award, Elmer turned to me and said, 'We got away with it.'

The Broadway show we wrote was called *Merlin* and all the signs were good – it looked as though we couldn't fail. The book writers were Richard Levinson and William Link, who wrote and created the television series *Columbo*. Chita Rivera was to star in it along with Doug Henning, who was a famous illusionist and magician. He played the part of the young Merlin. Also in the cast, although unknown at the time, were Nathan Lane and Christian Slater. I think it's fair to say that Doug Henning was probably the weirdest leading man I've ever worked with. He was a very spiritual person and meditated for most of the day. He wouldn't attend rehearsals until 2pm and then only stayed for an hour or so. He talked a lot about enlightenment. In New York at that time people just went along with his odd lifestyle. In England people would have said, 'He's bleedin' bonkers.'

It was explained to Doug that he would have to have singing lessons because the show was a musical. One day the creative team went to his singing teacher's house to see how he was doing. The word excruciating doesn't come close. All of us writers went into the garden and I said to them, 'Which way to the airport?' That got a great laugh. He was a sweet man but on a totally different planet. We never did go to the airport and my other suggestion was also ignored; I said to Elmer 'How about we lock him in his room with a bottle of Jack Daniels and a couple of hookers?'

There was a wonderful moment during rehearsals when Doug insisted that everyone attending would have to sign a confidentiality clause as how he performs his illusions is a secret and his illusions are valuable. So many things went wrong when he was trying to make some ducks disappear and again when he attempted to change an actress into a panther. Everyone could see how these illusions were done. Shirley said 'This will be the only opening night where the whole audience will have to sign a confidentiality clause!'

The show failed but it was not an embarrassment. It stumbled along for ten months on the Great White Way. The reviewer in the *New York Times* said that, 'Doug Henning may be able to make a panther disappear, what a shame he can't act his way out of a paper bag.' The big song from the show was thankfully sung by George Lee Andrews who did it beautifully. He played the part of Old Merlin, who dispensed his wisdom in spiritual terms with the song 'He Who Knows the Way'. I was surprised that no one asked the question how come the young Merlin couldn't sing a note, yet the old Merlin could sing to die for.

> So many people are lost in this world
> Running but going nowhere
> They reach for the stars
> But you can't reach the stars
> Unless you know how to get there . . .

THE SANEST GUY IN THE ROOM

He who knows the way
Has everything
More than eyes can see
Yes, everything
You've no need to go far
In fact you've no need to move my friend
For your dreams do not lie around some bend

No, there's a world inside of you
That you don't know
A spark you haven't found
That longs to glow and glow
All shadows go
Suddenly light is everywhere
Come follow he who knows the way
I'll take you there
Open up your mind
And you are there
So let go of the past
Tomorrow can wait
Your time is now

Someone must let you know
There's more to you than you can see
And I am he.

'True Grit'

One day little girl

The sadness will leave your face

As soon as we've won

Your fight to get justice done

Some days little girl

You'll wonder what life's about

But others have known

Few battles are won alone

So you'll look around to find

Someone who's kind

Someone who is fearless like you

The pain of it

Will ease a bit

When you find a man with true grit

One day you will rise

And you won't believe your eyes

You'll wake up and see

A world that is fine and free

Though summer seems far away

You will find the sun

One day.

| WORDS

That 'fuggertive' moment has followed me all of my life. When I worked at the *New Musical Express*, the editor, a man called Ray Sonin, used words like obviate and doleful. The chief reporter was a man called Mike Butcher. He used words like mordant and egregious. Mr Sonin and Mr Butcher kept me busy. I used to write these words down and search for simpler synonyms. I later came across that list and here are some of the words I repeated over and over again to myself in a vain attempt never to feel embarrassed again:

> Obviate – prevent
> Doleful – sad
> Mordant – biting/caustic
> Egregious – shocking/remarkable *enormity?*
> Protean – versatile
> Sapient – wise
> Timorous – fearful

I could probably fill the rest of this book with this extremely long list of hard-to-grasp words, but I've found that knowing the meaning of words has been a major asset. When you are mixing with writers and directors who are highly educated such as Trevor

Nunn, Richard Eyre, Stephen Fry and Christopher Hampton it doesn't bother you if they say the lyric sounds a bit sententious (preachy).

Marilyn Monroe said, 'Give the girl the right shoes and she can conquer the world.' I say give a man a beard and a good vocabulary and he's invincible.

> Johnny Mercer was watching a Henry Fonda movie and Fonda used the phrase 'Jeepers Creepers', which in those days in America was a more polite way of saying 'Jesus Christ'. He wrote the phrase down as lyric writers often do. It was a good job too because those two words fitted beautifully to Harry Warren's tune and gave Johnny his first Academy Award nomination. Unfortunately it lost to 'Thanks for the Memory' but it still did very nicely thank you.

| BORN FREE

It started out like any other song; John Barry played it rather badly on a piano in my office at NEMS. I asked him what the film was about and he said, 'It's about a lion called Elsa who is tamed and at the end she is set free to go into the wild.' That sort of said it all and I wrote:

> Born free
> As free as the wind blows
> As free as the grass grows
> Born free to follow your heart
>
> Live free
> And beauty surrounds you
> The world still astounds you
> Each time you look at a star
>
> Stay free
> Where no walls divide you
> You're free as the roaring tide
> So there's no need to hide
>
> Born free
> And life is worth living
> But only worth living
> 'Cos you're born free

John was very happy with what I came up with but the producer Carl Foreman wasn't. He thought the tune was too sentimental and syrupy, and the words were too much of a social comment. John said to Carl Foreman (as he also said to Harry Saltzman regarding 'Diamonds Are Forever'): 'What the fuck do you know about songs?'

I never had much to do with Mr. Foreman but John took an instant dislike to him. He found him, as he put it, 'Up his own arse.' We recorded the song with Matt Monro and the plan was that it would go at the end of the picture. However, Carl took it off the soundtrack and it didn't appear at the royal première of the film. This was highly embarrassing for Matt and his family as they told everyone that it was going to be featured. I regarded the whole episode as just another disappointment. As luck would have it, the pianist Roger Williams recorded the song with a choir and his record shot up the American hit parade. Columbia pictures, who published the song, realised that this could possibly be an Academy Award-winning song, but to make it eligible it would have to appear in every print of the movie. They then recalled every print and added Matt's vocal. It was now in the running for an Oscar. I had no idea of the Herculean effort that is made by everyone to get an Oscar nomination. A mountain of promotional marketing material is launched at every Academy member. It's a never-ending onslaught to try and gain their vote. Once you get a nomination the intensity of persuasion is palpably increased. We got the nomination and everyone was in a state of euphoria. The other nominees were pretty impressive: Bacharach and David with 'Alfie', Jim Dale and Tom Springfield with 'Georgy Girl', 'A Time for Love' by Johnny Mandel and Paul

Francis Webster, and 'Wishing Doll' by Elmer Bernstein and Mack David.

I personally thought that 'Alfie' was our biggest competition, but when I was sitting in the auditorium that night with Shirley I thought we had a good chance. The reason I changed my mind was because on the night it was sung by a multi-ethnic choir. The song seemed to speak out to oppressed people around the planet. Dean Martin was the star who read out the nominations and said the words that changed all our lives: 'The winner is John Barry and Don Black for "Born Free".' At the after-show party Carl Foreman came up to me and said 'Well, it does grow on you.'

When we got back to our hotel on Sunset Boulevard the staff were lined up and applauded as we entered. There were Champagne, flowers and fruit in our rooms from Columbia Pictures and the telegrams began to arrive from everyone I had ever met. My sister Nita called me to say that she saw an *Evening Standard* placard that read: East End boy wins Oscar.

When all this excitement died down I heard from some very grumpy people who said I thanked the wrong person in my speech. I had been told by Screen Gems, who published 'Born Free', that, in the case I should win, I must thank Donnie Kirshner, who ran the company. I did this and then I had a call from a frightening-looking man called Jonie Taps (you don't get names like that in England) who ran the movie side of the company. He said to me: 'Why did you thank that cocksucker!?' He said *he* was responsible for the success of the song. I told him I would thank him next time, I don't think he smiled.

I had no idea that to get a name check on this show was so important. I do now.

WHEN WILL IT FALL THROUGH?

For as long as I can remember my sons Grant and Clive have had a realistic approach to their careers, perhaps forced upon them by me. Grant will say to me one day, 'Dad, great news! I think I may have the next Mariah Carey single.' He will then say, 'It won't fall through for at least three weeks.' This means he has three glorious weeks of dreaming that it could happen. Clive will often say, 'I had a wonderful meeting today about running a record company in New York, I won't know it's off for another week.' I also say things like, 'There's talk about me writing with the great composer John Kander because his regular lyricist Fred Ebb died.' They will both say back to me, almost in unison, 'When will it fall through?' Having this attitude takes a lot of the nail-biting stress out of our lives because so many things do fall through and if you've trained your mind to half expect them to, you're quids in. Our delusions are what keep us going.

This kind of attitude is just one of the tools I use to help me bounce back time and again from failed ventures. That, and Shirley's philosophy of, 'Who cares, as long as we're all healthy,' plus my snooker fixation have shielded me from ever even thinking of turning it all in.

Snooker is more of a meditation than a sport. I don't know why I get so engrossed but I do. The elation when a ball drops in that netted pocket, the mortification when you miss a black off the spot. Ronnie O'Sullivan made the maximum break of 147 in about five minutes; it sometimes takes me and my partner twenty minutes to pot the first red. The other thing I love about the game is you don't even have to know the person you're playing with. You both know why you're there and what you're trying to do so you can spend an hour or two with someone in close proximity and not utter a word.

I've played with the great Jimmy White, who is known as the whirlwind. He gave me a seventy-five start and still beat me. I was thrilled when he gave me his cue as a present. Unfortunately none of his skill came with it. I once said to him jokingly that I find it hard to get more than an eighty break and his deadpan reply was, 'Don't matter, as long as you enjoy the game.'

Snooker came to my rescue one difficult day in New York, when I was working on the musical *Merlin*. I had been up half the night with Elmer Bernstein writing a song for our leading man Doug Henning. I was sitting in the stalls of the Mark Hellinger theatre with Elmer and Richard Levinson, one of the book writers of the show. Richard was having a lousy day as he had just come back from the doctor who diagnosed that he had Bell's palsy. This a condition that causes temporary paralysis to one side of your face. His mouth was vertical where it should have been horizontal. He was very depressed about it, and after listening to Doug Henning attempt to sing our song, and fail miserably, the three of us wanted to run out of there. I came up with the idea of going to my hideaway, the New York Athletic Club on Central Park South. Richard and Elmer sat drinking while I played endless frames of snooker with the club's marker.

By the time I had finished I had potted my way out of all my dark clouds. They both staggered out feeling just as bad as when they went in but I left feeling fresh and renewed. If snooker is an addiction it's the most harmless one to choose. When I watch it on television I can stay up half the night, it can really be edge-of-the-seat drama to equal Hitchcock's *Psycho*. I'm hooked from the start with the stirring music as the players are introduced by their flamboyant nicknames: The Rocket (Ronnie O'Sullivan), Enter the Dragon (Ding Junhui), The Juddernaught (Judd Trump), The Hawk (Barry Hawkins), The Thunder from Down Under (Neil Robertson). I think this nicknaming began with Alex Higgins who was introduced as The Hurricane. Another thing I like about this sport on television is the way the winner of a tournament is paid there and then. They are handed an envelope with their cheque inside, as if it comes from a kind uncle. It's all so gentlemanly and civilised.

I FILLED OUT THE FORMS

I loved to make Shirley laugh. I remember saying to her one night in bed just before I turned the light out, 'You're a lovely lady but I can see how you wouldn't appeal to everyone.' This became a line she often quoted over the years. She always went to bed ten minutes before me no matter how tired she was. She had to puff up the cushions, put the cups in the dishwasher and empty the kettle. She always left her phone book by the kitchen telly. It still sits there and always will. As soon as something breaks, I open it and there is always the name of a person who will fix it. When I had to find a key the gardener needed I had no idea where to look, but I opened a drawer and found an envelope clearly marked 'key for garden padlock'.

We never spoke much about dying. She used to say to me, 'If you go first I'll kill you.' And 'If I go first you'll never be able to fill out the forms.'

I spend a lot of time with my sons these days and I get a sense that the three of us constantly avoid mentioning her in case we upset ourselves or spoil the evening. Just like a game of snooker where you don't have to say a word to know how your partner feels. I know, and they know, Shirley had gifts we've never seen in anyone else.

| BEN

Some people have glittering careers but remain unknown to the wider public. Such a person was Walter Scharf. He was the man with whom I wrote my first musical, *Maybe That's Your Problem*. This is the musical that is never mentioned in either of our CVs! During his illustrious career he received eleven Oscar nominations and four Emmys. He scored over two hundred pictures including *Funny Girl*, *Hans Christian Andersen* and *Willy Wonka and the Chocolate Factory*. He also scored films starring Elvis Presley and Dean Martin and Jerry Lewis. Walter called me one day in 1971 and said he was doing a minor film that was being produced by Bing Crosby Productions (yes, that Bing Crosby) and they needed a song in it. I asked him what it was about and he told me over the phone that the movie was called *Ben* and Ben is a rat who befriends a young boy who is very ill with leukaemia! So, we have to write a song about a rat? He said, 'You wrote one about a lion, what's the difference?' It sounded a daunting prospect, that is until I met with Walter and he played me this gorgeous melody. I saw two brief clips from the film, one where the boy is unhappy and distressed and another when he is playing and laughing with this friendly rat. I realised then that I couldn't write a lyric about cheese or traps, but I could write one about friendship. The tune was so lovely that the words came easily:

Ben, the two of us need look no more
We both found what we were looking for
With a friend to call my own
I'll never be alone
And you my friend will see
You've got a friend in me

Ben, you're always running here and there
You feel you're not wanted anywhere
If you ever look behind
And don't like what you find
There's something you should know
You've got a place to go
I used to say I and me
Now it's us
Now it's we

Ben, most people would turn you away
I don't listen to a word they say
They don't see you as I do
I wish they would try to
I'm sure they'd think again
If they had a friend like Ben
Like Ben

Walter loved it and so did the studio. Now all we had to do was find someone to sing it. Lots of names were mentioned including Donny Osmond. Michael Jackson's name came up because he was the hottest singer around as part of the Jackson Five. He had just announced that he was going solo. A meeting was arranged for us to meet Michael at Walter's studio in Brentwood, a fashionable area of Beverly Hills. He arrived with his father Joe and a couple of heavy-looking minders.

Michael sat next to Walter on the piano seat as he played the tune and I sort of spoke/sang the lyric. There was a wonderful reaction from Michael and before long he was singing it. He particularly loved the lyric of the middle section:

> I used to say
> I and me
> Now it's us
> Now it's we.

Later on in his autobiography he wrote that they were his favourite lines of any of the songs he'd sung. His record of 'Ben' shot up to number one in the American charts and was nominated for an Oscar. Michael sang the song at the Academy ceremony. I got to know Michael very well throughout this period and he was a joy to be with. He was only fourteen and as innocent as any normal kid of that age. When I moved to Los Angeles in 1974 we became even closer. We rented a house on Somera Road in Bel Air and Michael would come and swim and play pool with my sons Grant and Clive. Shirley was learning to paint at that time and she and Michael did a drawing together of a Mexican peasant. This drawing became one of our most prized possessions. I had the most surprising conversations with Michael about songs. He told me his favourite song was 'Inchworm' from *Hans Christian Andersen*, and he sang it to us all around the pool table.

155

I told him about Frank Loesser, the man who wrote that song and said he also wrote a couple of my favourite songs – 'Baby It's Cold Outside' and 'Slow Boat to China'. He wrote the titles down and said he would check them out. I also had a tenuous link to Michael because his best friend at school was the son of Johnny Spence who was Matt Monro's musical director for many years. Michael was fascinated by the fact that Matt was a bus driver from Shoreditch and had such a beautiful voice. I talked to him about Matt for many hours.

One night I'll never forget was the night we went to a party at the Beverly Wilshire Hotel. Michael was in great form and he introduced us to Sophia Loren. My old pal Petula Clark was also there. When we sat down I was next to the Hollywood actress Evelyn Keyes. She played Al Jolson's wife in the film *The Jolson Story*. This is a film I loved to bits as a kid and I saw it over thirty times. I was so excited to meet her. I told her this and she said to me, 'Yeah, I saw it recently on television about three in the morning, what a load of hogwash.' That took me ages to get over. Sometimes it doesn't pay to meet your heroes.

One day I got a phone call from Michael's father saying that if I or my family wanted to speak to Michael I would have to go through him. It really shocked us all because every time he came over we all had such a fun time – particularly Michael. I never called his father and Michael and I sort of drifted.

A few years later Michael would call me when he was in London and ask me if I would like to ride around town with him. He usually called late at night and the last thing I wanted to do was to go out to show him Big Ben. I did get a call from him one day when he asked me and Walter Scharf to write some children's songs for him. He loved the songs and paid us handsomely for writing them. I understand that he did make demos of them and I hope one day they will be found.

We also met again at another glittering Hollywood party and when we reminisced about those pool-playing days in Bel Air a huge smile beamed across his face. It was a smile that was smiled less frequently as the years went by.

ANDREW ... MYSTERY MAN

The two questions I am asked most frequently are, 'What comes first, the words or the music?' and, 'What is Andrew Lloyd Webber really like?' Well, considering he's the most successful composer in the world he is remarkably well balanced. Unlike Van Gogh he still has both ears and unlike Ernest Hemingway he's never reached for a shotgun. By the time I met him in 1978 I had already won an Oscar and a Golden Globe, had two American number ones and written a bunch of James Bond theme songs. More importantly, I had written a successful musical called *Billy* and I had also written a musical with Broadway's Jule Styne. The reason I mention this is because I had no cause to be intimidated by him. Andrew was most impressed with my theatrical leanings which led to our many collaborations. Although my career was going well it was enhanced beyond words when I wrote with Andrew.

He has been accused of being a megalomaniac, a plagiarist, a liar, a cheat, a dictator, toxic, bonkers – and that's just by his family and friends! I joke, of course. What he is is unusual. Imagine if Jeff Bezos of Amazon could also sing the lead in Verdi's *La Traviata* at the Metropolitan Opera House in New York. Andrew is a man of many talents and moods but he is also, as I've said earlier, great company and thrilling to write with. He has the ability to forget his role as a theatre or property owner when he is composing. For many years he created the Sydmonton Festival, which took place in one of his magnificent homes. There was always a frivolous debate on arcane subjects. I used to chair this debate and it was a chance to have fun with the many celebrated guests. I did this in the style of a Friars roast that I'd seen so often on my trips to New York. I remember introducing the politician David Mellor as, 'A man who is difficult to hate but well worth the effort.' But I think I got the biggest laugh when I said, 'You have to admire Andrew, if you don't you're fired!' Andrew laughed the loudest and I think quite likes being 'roasted'. I once said, 'I've been given two minutes to sing Andrew's praises which is considerably more time than I need ... '

When it comes to the actual writing of lyrics Andrew has an immediate response and he's usually right. He knows so much about so many things and yet I've never seen him read a book. I'm not sure he ever has. Unusual? You bet.

| SAM

When we were living in Los Angeles I got to know John Farrar, who was one of the guitarists with Cliff Richard's Shadows. He and Hank Marvin had come up with a gorgeous tune. John's wife, Pat, had just had a baby they called Sam. That's where I came in. The tune needed a one-word title, and the name Sam sang beautifully on that note. Pat Farrar's best friend was Olivia Newton John. She heard the song, loved it and recorded it. It went to number one in America's easy listening chart. It turned out to be one of my favourite records. It's a funny thing but after Ben was such a big hit parents started to call their sons Ben. The same thing happened with Sam, although Sam works for boys and girls.

> I heard that you're on your own now
>
> So am I
>
> I'm living alone now
>
> I was wrong
>
> So were you
>
> What will you do?
>
> Are you glad to be free?
>
> Are you feeling lost
>
> Just like me?

SAM

Longing for company

Oh, Sam, Sam

You know where I am

Come around and talk awhile

I need your smile

You need a shoulder

Oh, Sam, Sam

You know where I am

And the door is open wide

Come on inside

Longing to see you

Oh Sam, Sam

You know where I am

I find the days hard to face now

Empty rooms

There's much too much space now

And the nights go so slow

I'm sure you know

Wish I knew

What to do

It would be so nice

Seeing you

And it might

Help you too

Oh Sam, Sam

You know where I am

Come around and talk awhile

I need your smile

THE SANEST GUY IN THE ROOM

You need a shoulder

Oh Sam, Sam

You know where I am

And the door is open wide

Come on inside

Longing to see you

Oh Sam, Sam

You know where I am

THE ODD COUPLES

Many years ago Shirley and I went to stay at the La Samanna Hotel on the Caribbean island of St Martin. It seemed that all the other guests were old men accompanied by young girls. The manager of the hotel said to us, 'We refer to them as uncles and nieces.' Shirley felt very uncomfortable seeing these oddly matched couples. I am reminded of this now that I am an older man and on my own. Shirley used to think that these 'uncles' at the hotel went with young girls for the sex. That is far from the truth. During the last eighteen months I have been on dinner dates with older women and younger women. There are pluses and minuses on both sides. Now I am in my eighties I don't expect to find someone who will run breathlessly into my arms through a golden cornfield, but I know that Shirley wouldn't want me to be alone.

I've had some delightful evenings with women in their sixties and seventies and sooner or later the conversation inevitably turns to health issues. Throughout the meal words like fibrillation, blood thinners, arthritis, memory loss and hip replacements usually make an appearance. And as you would expect you also talk about their grandchildren and their topsy-turvy past that has led them to having dinner with a man in his eighties. When you're with a mature lady you can't help being aware of your own mortality. I had dinner recently with Debbie Wiseman, a frequent musical collaborator of mine. When I told her about my afore-mentioned views she made me laugh out loud when she said, 'Whatever you do, never go on *Loose Women*.' For those of you who have never seen this television show it is a daily look at life from a woman's point of view.

However, there are many pluses in spending time with someone from your own generation. For a start they have heard of Frankie Laine and Harold Wilson and know most of the words to 'It Had to Be You'. Also, they have known joy and heartache and, in most cases, love and loss. You can relate to each other on so many levels as you are in the same boat, so to speak.

When you have dinner with a much younger lady you are talking to someone who has had an unlived life, has firmer skin but not firm opinions. They allow you to remind yourself of how you were when you were in your prime, and that is a wonderful feeling. They also see you as wiser and more romantic which is no bad thing for your ego. On the minus side you cannot keep up this charade for long. It's exhausting trying to avoid phrases that will leave her looking confused and you feeling like a relic from a bygone era. Phrases like 'A fly in the ointment' or 'A nod is as good as a wink' or ' That's a turn-up for the books.'

The theatrical producer Michael Harrison has a lovely young wife called Kathryn. Recently she invited me to be her plus-one to a Robbie Williams concert. I have never felt so old in my life. Everyone, and I mean everyone, in the audience stood up the whole time and screamed and waved their arms throughout the evening. I tried sitting down but felt an idiot when I realised I was the only one who was. I am a Robbie Williams fan but I couldn't take it and left very early. Kathryn stayed and the next day told me she had one of the best nights of her life.

My old friend Alan Jay Lerner wrote a song called 'I'm Glad I'm Not Young Anymore' from the musical *Gigi* and I've chosen some lines from it which say it all really:

> And even if love comes through the door
> The kind that goes on forevermore
> Forevermore is shorter than before
> I'm glad I'm not young anymore

BOMBAY DREAMS

Andrew Lloyd Webber went crazy when he heard the music of A. R. Rahman. He saw a Bollywood movie that Rahman had scored and checked out his other work. I remember Andrew saying, 'He's one of the best melodists of all time.' Rahman has been called 'The Mozart of Madras' and is as big as you can get with the Asian population. I found this out when I went walking with him in London and then to the Bombay Brasserie, a fashionable Indian restaurant in Kensington. You would have thought that Elvis Presley and Frank Sinatra had walked in together. The response was practically biblical. He doesn't have fans, he has disciples and followers.

Andrew wanted him to write a musical and thought that he needed to work with someone who was patient and experienced in musicals. That's where I came in. The musical was *Bombay Dreams*, and it was both a dream and a nightmare to work on. Rahman had never written a musical and had no idea that songs had to be written to a schedule. He is very religious and prays five times a day. Often in the middle of writing a song he would disappear for an hour without telling me that he'd be out for a while. I remember walking with him to some meeting in Soho and we had to pass a bunch of sex shops and strip joints to get there. As soon as we returned he prayed so that he could cleanse his spirit. Faith plays an all-important role in his life. I was so frustrated one day that I felt like asking him to pray for a chorus.

I have always preferred to work in the mornings but he prefers to work late and into the night. He never wrote a complete song. He gave me a cassette of what he called 'jamming sessions', and I would listen endlessly to these fragments of tunes, picking bits of one that I liked and trying to marry it with another bit on the tape. I felt like I was a song detective during this process.

As time went on I got used to this way of working. I've never written so many songs without my shoes on. There were times when I thought this show could never happen as the music was painfully slow in coming. I would give him a title and if he liked it he would make a call to get an orchestra in that night as well as singers. I would say, 'but we only have a title!' Somehow or other when he did get a bunch of musicians together something magical always happened. When I tried to push him he would say in a calming voice, 'It will happen when it's meant to happen.' He is often called a genius. But once when he called me at three in the morning Shirley said, 'If he's such a genius why can't he tell the fucking time!'

The lyrics to Bollywood songs are filled with romantic and mystical poetry. So I read a lot of Eastern poetry books by Rumi and I really enjoyed entering this idealised world. I wrote lines that I would never normally write:

> Everyone needs a sense of belonging
> Someone there who always understands
> That precious gifts can come from empty hands

Those words are from the song 'How Many Stars'. The hit song from the show was 'Shakalaka Baby', but my favourite is 'The Journey Home Is Never Too Long'. Again, a universal thought in the title:

The journey home is never too long
Your heart arrives before the train
The journey home is never too long
Some yesterdays always remain
I'm going back to when my heart was light
When my pillow was a ship
I sailed through the night

Not every road you come across
Is one you have to take
No, sometimes standing still can be
The best move you ever make

The journey home is never too long
Home helps to heal
The deepest pain
The journey home is never too long
Your heart arrives before the train
The journey home is never too long
When open arms are waiting there
The journey home is never too long
There's room to love and room to spare
I want to feel the way that I did then
I'll think my wishes through
Before I wish again

The show ran for two years in London and there is talk of bringing it back. I would love to work with Rahman again. His outlook on life has rubbed off on me a little. I still like to work in the mornings and I prefer to work with a completed melody. But when an uptight producer is screaming for a song I quietly think to myself, 'It will happen when it's meant to happen.'

DONALD ZEC

Donald Zec was 101 years old on 12 March 2020. He was the legendary Entertainment reporter with the *Daily Mirror* in the fifties. He lives just a seven-minute walk from me and his wise and witty company has been cherished by Shirley and me for quite a few years now. Donald has sailed with Humphrey Bogart, fallen out with Frank Sinatra and taken 4 a.m. calls from Marilyn Monroe. What makes him stand out from other elderly people is his humour and lack of self-pity. I called him recently to ask him how he was, he said, 'I'm fine. You're lucky to catch me in.' Another day I called to see how he was doing and he said, 'I feel a little tired today,' he paused and said, 'If I'm like this now God knows what I'll be like when I'm older.'

He is one of the world's finest satirical writers. He once wrote this about the Hollywood actress Gloria Grahame, 'She has been called man hungry, but if she wasn't man hungry she was certainly peckish.' Once, when he was flying alongside Marilyn Monroe to Phoenix, Arizona, the stewardess put a tray of food on Marilyn's lap. 'Oh, no thank you, honey,' she said, 'I have to watch my figure.' Donald, ever helpful, said, 'Why don't you eat the food, my dear and I'll watch your figure.' He once asked her what she would like on her tombstone: 'Here lies Marilyn Monroe, 38-23-36,' she said.

When his wife of sixty-six years died in 2006 Donald had to find a hobby or two. Since then he has learned to paint and won *The Oldie* magazine's British Artists Award for the over-sixties. A year later a portrait of his grandfather was presented at The Royal Academy Summer Exhibition, jointly winning the Hugh Casson prize for drawing. When he got to the podium to collect his award he looked at his speech then put it away saying, 'I won't bother with that, it only says do not resuscitate.'

Donald has also learned to play a few classical pieces on the piano. He's been a great help to me in writing this memoir. He keeps telling me just to get it all down, there'll be time to tweak it later. He loved Shirley and Shirley loved him. He has given me great strength during my grief and turned himself into an inspirational role model. The Booker-Prize-winning author Howard Jacobson is a friend and a huge fan. He has said that many of their conversations together have influenced his writing. When the James Bond producer Cubby Broccoli died Donald became a surrogate father to his daughter Barbara. She has been centre stage in his life ever since.

Like everyone who lives to an old age he has not gone unmarked. He has his medical issues. When he walks it is with a frame. He is also blind in one eye and suffers from insomnia. I told him when Shirley passed that I needed to take sleeping pills now and then although I know they're no good for me. He said in that comforting way of his, 'You're eighty years old, become a fucking addict.'

| TOMORROW NEVER DIES

In 1996, I had a call from the composer David Arnold. He asked me a very stupid question: Would I like to work on the new Bond film? Before you could say the word Blofeld we were in the same room. Unlike John Barry, David likes to look at a few lyric ideas. He's very good at talking you through the story and from his summary I came back with a bunch of random thoughts. We came up with a first draft of the song and he made a demo with him singing. This was a wow moment for me because I've never worked with a composer who could sing to die for. His voice is extraordinary, a cross between Jack Jones, Tony Bennett and Don McLean. He could sing 'Happy Birthday' and you would be moved.

We were very happy with the song we came up with and were disappointed when we learned that the studio wanted a major rock star to sing the main title theme. I found out later on that a few writers had a go at it including Simon Le Bon and Jarvis Cocker. In the end the studio went for Sheryl Crow who couldn't have been hotter at that time. Sheryl, like most performers now, writes her own material and she came up with the title song. Our song was used as the end-title and it was sung beautifully by k. d. lang. We couldn't have two songs called 'Tomorrow Never Dies' so I had to modify ours. We changed the title to 'Surrender' so that people wouldn't be confused, although the words 'tomorrow never dies' feature a lot in 'Surrender'.

Your life is a story

I've already written

The news is that I am in control

And I have the power to make you surrender

Not only your body but your soul

Tomorrow never dies . . . surrender

Tomorrow will arrive on time

I'll tease and tantalise

With every line

Till you are mine

Tomorrow never dies

Whatever you're after

Trust me, I'll deliver

You'll relish the world that I create

Tomorrow never dies . . . surrender

Tomorrow will arrive on time

I'll tease and tantalise

With every line

Till you are mine

Tomorrow never dies

The truth is now

What I say

I've taken care of yesterday

Tomorrow never dies . . . surrender

Tomorrow will arrive on time

THE SANEST GUY IN THE ROOM

I'll tease and tantalise

With every line

Till you are mine

Tomorrow never dies

Tomorrow never dies

Tomorrow never dies

CARE HOMES

We never talked about dying but we did talk about care homes quite a bit. Shirley's dad was in The Nightingale which is about as good as care homes get. I've also spoken at many of these places and they do a fantastic job in keeping the aged busy and curious about what's going on in the world. Some of these homes are visited by terrific entertainers who perform for the residents in the afternoon or evening and it's the highlight of their week. Many well-known stars like Maureen Lipman are regular visitors. Whenever I'm with my sons and get someone's name wrong they will say, 'Don't worry, Dad, the entertainer's coming tonight!' It always amazed me and Shirley how people with dementia and other crippling diseases become happier when they were singing old songs. Shirley came across a poem once that was in the *Daily Mail*, which she cut out and I found the other day.

'Moving to a Care Home'
There's an old chap come to our care home,
Rather quiet, but quite nicely dressed
Keeps himself to himself most of the time
He needs time to get settled I guessed
Someone said, 'He's a very good pianist.'
We've a Steinway he might like to play.

175

THE SANEST GUY IN THE ROOM

Who knows we might have a sing-song,
That would certainly brighten our day.'
Do you think he could play some Glenn Miller?
Or maybe some Irving Berlin?
'We'll Meet Again' or the 'White Cliffs of Dover'
Or 'When They Begin the Beguine'?
We certainly don't need any song sheets
Word perfect we'll be, don't you fret,
There might be things we just can't remember
Words of songs, though, we never forget.
I'm not sure what the next generation will sing
When they're in a care home like me,
I doubt very much if they'll have a sing-song
So they won't know how great it can be.
You see that is the problem with pop songs,
They come and go quick as a flash,
Just like the singers and most of the bands
Number one for a week and then . . . crash!
So what are the poor fans left with?
Nothing memorable, Beatles maybe,
But they don't have the lyrics and melodies we had,
Nor the memories, like you and me.
So I hope the new bloke can be tempted,
He's maybe just waiting the chance,
I bet if he played us a St. Bernard Waltz,
We'd jump out of our wheelchairs and dance!

John Stenhouse (aged 90)
Blyth, Northumberland.

ASPECTS OF LOVE

I wrote earlier about trying to come up with a universal thought when writing a song. Thankfully that's what happened when I was in the middle of writing the musical *Aspects of Love* with Andrew Lloyd Webber and Charles Hart. When Andrew played the tune the title 'Love Changes Everything' came almost immediately. There is a genuine truth to this song, which is also a great asset – everyone can relate to it because love really does change everything. The song became a huge hit for Michael Ball and kicked off his well-deserved fame and fortune. *Aspects of Love* was also a hit and ran for almost three years. At this time Prince Edward was working for The Really Useful Company and he would make me the odd cup of tea! Looking back that all seems a bit surreal. He would drop me memos asking for my biog or a photo and sign them Edward Windsor.

I have fond memories of chatting with Roger Moore who was scheduled to star in the leading role. He was very witty and charming, cynical and subtle. He famously resigned from the show because he said he wasn't confident enough to play the part eight times a week. I always felt he was terrific and sang very well. I used to know his ex-wife Dorothy Squires very well from my Denmark Street days. She was very loud and very vulgar but a remarkable entertainer. It was not a match made in heaven.

The show, unfortunately, was not received as well in New York. It was reviewed by Frank Rich of the *New York Times* who was known as 'The Butcher of Broadway'. At the first-night party I said to Andrew and our director Trevor Nunn that I would be delighted if he only hates it! I remember looking at Andrew's bloodless face as he was reading the review. It was one of those nights to remember and impossible to forget. In spite of Mr Rich's blood-curdling report the show ran for almost a year.

I wrote the lyrics for the show with Charles Hart, who also wrote the lyrics to *The Phantom of the Opera*. We did enjoy writing the piece and I remember many silly dinners the three of us had in and around Cap Ferrat. I say silly because we played a game that may sound childish now but at the time had Andrew, Charles and myself in hysterics. The game was to sub- stitute the last word of a song title with the word arsehole. This produced titles like My Funny A*******, That Old Black A*******, It Never Entered My A*******, I'm Gonna Wash That Man Right Out Of My A*******, I've Grown Accustomed To Her A*******, I Wonder Who's Kissing Her A*******. This diversion kept us amused after a long day discussing the Bloomsbury Set and their complicated romantic liaisons. Dorothy Parker was quoted as saying about them, 'They lived in squares, painted in circles, and loved in triangles.'

I'm often asked how you work with another lyricist. Well, I've done this quite a few times with playwright Christopher Hampton. We worked on *Sunset Boulevard*, *Dracula*, *Stephen Ward* and the upcoming *The Third Man*. The trick to it is to get in the habit of thinking aloud. You have to be brutally honest with each other; if you think his idea stinks or he thinks the

same about yours you have to say so, there's no time to walk on
eggshells.

Love,

Love changes everything

Hands and faces

Earth and sky

Love,

Love changes everything

How you live and,

How you die,

Love,

Can make the summer fly,

Or a night,

Seem like a lifetime,

Yes, love,

Love changes everything,

Now I tremble,

At your name,

Nothing in the world

Will ever

Be the same

Love,

Love changes everything,

Days are longer,

Words mean more,

Love,

THE SANEST GUY IN THE ROOM

Love changes everything,
Pain is deeper, Than before

Love,
Will turn your world around
And that world, Will last forever,

Yes, love,
Love changes everything,
Brings you glory,
Brings you shame,
Nothing in the world
Will ever be the same

Off into the world we go,
Planning futures,
Shaping years,
Love bursts in and suddenly,
All our wisdom Disappears,

Love,
Makes fools of everyone,
All the rules
We make are broken,

Yes, love,
Love changes everyone,
Live or perish,
In its flame,

ASPECTS OF LOVE

> Love will never,
> Never let you
> Be the same

Although 'Love Changes Everything' was the big commercial hit from the show, in the theatre the one that got the biggest applause was, in my opinion, a far superior song. It's what people call the 11 o'clock number and comes when our leading lady is all alone after her husband George has died and her young lover Alex has left her. During the show she hints at her fear of being alone and sings 'Anything But Lonely'.

> Anything but lonely,
> Anything but empty rooms,
> There's so much in life to share,
> What's the sense if no one else is there?
>
> Anything but lonely,
> Anything but only me,
> Quiet years in too much space,
> That's the thing that's hard to face
> You have the right to go,
> But you should also know,
> I won't be alone for long.
>
> Long days with nothing said,
> Are not what lies ahead,
> I'm sorry but I'm not that strong.

181

THE SANEST GUY IN THE ROOM

Anything but lonely,

Anything but passing time,

Lonely's what I'll never be,

While there's still some life in me,

And I'm still young don't forget,

It isn't over yet,

So many hearts for me to thrill.

If you're not here to say

How good I look each day,

I'll have to find someone who will.

Anything but lonely,

Anything but empty rooms,

There's so much in life to share,

What's the sense when no one else is there.

| THE ITALIAN JOB

I was thrilled to be working with the musical icon Quincy Jones on this wonderful film. I had admired him for years; the man has won twenty-seven Grammy Awards! Without doubt one of the greatest record producers, conductors and arrangers the world has ever known. However, what I came to learn was that he is not a natural songwriter. Our brief was to write a couple of songs, one being a romantic summery ballad and the other being some kind of novelty number. We met at the flat he was renting near Marble Arch and we started talking about the ballad. I thought it was going to be simple to come up with a catchy, sunny kind of song like 'Arriverderci Roma' or 'Volare'. Quincy, or Q, as he likes to be called, didn't have a tune in his trunk, so to speak, so we were starting from scratch. After he stared at the piano for about an hour, I suggested I pop out and come back in a while. I did this and came back hoping he'd have something, but it was not to be. I then suggested I come up with a few lines to get him started. Eventually I gave him:

> On days like these
> When skies are blue and fields are green

I left him with those lines, went over the park, and when I came back he had written just two notes! So we had the words and music to:

> On days

I came back the following day and he had written the most magnificent melody and I was delighted with it. I realised that he found it difficult to write something so simple as he had been working with the most sophisticated jazz artistes of all time: Sarah Vaughan, Billie Holiday, Count Basie, the list goes on and on. 'On Days Like These' happens to be one of my favourite songs and also the most requested one on my radio show:

> On days like these
> When skies are blue and fields are green
> I look around and think about what might have been
> And then I hear sweet music float around my head
> As I recall the many things we left unsaid
> It's on days like these that I remember
> Singing songs and drinking wine
> While your eyes played games with mine
>
> On days like these
> I wonder what became of you
> Maybe today you're singing songs
> With someone new
> I like to think you're walking by
> Those willow trees

> Remembering the love we knew
> On days like these

The other song we wrote for the film was so much fun to write because Q knew nothing about Cockney rhyming slang. Well, you wouldn't if you were born on the South Side of Chicago. He would fall about laughing at phrases like 'apples and pears' or 'put on your daisy roots'. For some reason I haven't been able to figure out why this song is often sung at football matches. One of the most stupid questions I've been asked by a reporter was, 'Did Quincy write the lyric?'

> This is the self-preservation society
> Go wash your German bands,
> Your boat race too
> Comb your Barnet Fair
> We got lots to do
> Put on your Dicky Dirt and your Peckham Rye
> Cause time's soon hurryin' by
> Get your skates on mate
> Get your skates on mate
> No bib around your Gregory Peck today, eh?
> Drop your plates of meat
> Right up on the seat
> This is the self-preservation society
> This is the self-preservation society
> Gotta get a bloomin' move on
> Babadab-babadabadab-bab
> Jump in the jam jar, gotta get straight

Hurry up mate

Don't wanna be late

How's your father?

Tiggety boo

Gotta get a bloomin' move on

Self-preservation society

This is the self-preservation society

Jump in the jam jar, gotta get straight

Hurry up mate

Don't wanna be late

How's your father?

Tickety boo, tickety boo

How's your father

Gotta get a bloomin' move on.

had dinner recently with Michael Caine and his very beautiful wife Shakira. We talked a lot about his early days when he shared a flat in London with John Barry. On his first night he got into bed and was looking forward to a good night's kip, as he put it. But as soon as his head hit the pillow John started playing the piano and never stopped all night. In the morning a bleary-eyed Michael said to him, 'You kept playing the same three notes all blinkin' night, what was it?' John said, 'It's the tune I've written for my new film called *Goldfinger*.'

I also asked Michael if he had a favourite song and he instantly said, 'My Way'. He explained why. When he was living in France he got to know the French composer and singer Claude Francois who wrote the original version. Later on he got to know Paul Anka very well who wrote the English lyric and after that he became great friends with Frank Sinatra who had a massive hit with the song. Great story, and as Michael could have said, 'Not a lot of people know that.'

THE WORLD IS NOT ENOUGH

I wrote this with David Arnold and it was my fifth Bond song. It was the one I had the most trouble with in coming up with the second line. I stared out of windows and walked through my usual parks where something generally pops into my head. One day Shirley opened the post and called out to me, 'Don, you've got an OBE! You've just got a letter, it's wonderful news.' I said, 'Well it's not a knighthood but it's a good place to start.' Then I thought that's my second line! The world is not enough but it's the perfect place to start. I was happier about that second line than I was about getting the OBE. The song was sung by Shirley Manson from the popular group Garbage.

I know how to hurt
I know how to heal
I know what to show
And what to conceal

I know when to talk
I know when to touch
No one ever died
From wanting too much

THE WORLD IS NOT ENOUGH

The world is not enough
But it is such a perfect place to start my love
And if you're strong enough
Together we can take the world apart my love

People like us know how to survive
There's no point in living
If you can't feel alive

We know when to kiss
And we know when to kill
If we can't have it all
Then nobody will

The world is not enough
But it is such a perfect place to start my love
And if you're strong enough
Together we can take the world apart my love

I feel safe
I feel scared
I feel ready
And yet unprepared

The world is not enough
But it is such a perfect place to start my love
And if you're strong enough
Together we can take the world apart my love
The world is not enough
The world is not enough
No, nowhere near enough
The world is not enough

189

YOU CAN'T HAVE ONE WITHOUT THE OTHER

A lyric isn't good unless it takes five legal-sized yellow pads and an entire box of Blackwing pencils to write.
Stephen Sondheim

Writing lyrics for musicals is a painful business, so much so that I once compared it to doing your own root canal work. This remark was received with a heartfelt sense of understanding by my fellow practitioners, Tim Rice, Herbert Kretzmer, Lionel Bart and Richard Stilgoe. Lyric writing is an elusive craft.

Often when critics review musicals they find it hard to devote more than a word or two to the lyrical contribution. The most dismissive words used are: banal, trite and serviceable or crisp, lively and sharp. Lyricists, on the whole, are raised to live with a great deal of anonymity. This can be attributed to years of careless disc jockey introductions: 'That was Henry Mancini's "Moon River" . . . Elton John's "Candle in the Wind" . . . Duke Ellington's "Do Nothing Till You Hear From Me".' No mention of Johnny Mercer, Bernie Taupin or Bob Russell.

Now, being overlooked by strangers is one thing, but to be overlooked by collaborators is unforgiveable. Many times I've squirmed in my seat when Burt Bacharach and Neil Sedaka hardly mention their lyrical collaborators. I'm pleased to say they don't do that any more. Burt has Hal David to thank for the words and Neil has Howard Greenfield. As Sammy Cahn said in his song 'Love and Marriage', 'You can't have one without the other.'

When Johnny Mercer was asked how he felt when his song was introduced as 'Henry Mancini's "Moon River"', he said, 'There's nothing you can do about it, it's like being ugly.'

It's a known fact that book writers of musicals don't get the credit they deserve either. Howard Lindsay and Russell Crouse were entitled to get a little peeved every time they read, 'That was Irving Berlin's "Call Me Madam"' or 'Rodger's and Hammerstein's "The Sound of Music"', because they were responsible for writing those monster hits. Somehow or other the book writer tends to get overlooked. This came vividly to mind a few years ago when I was writing *Bonnie and Clyde*. The composer Frank Wildhorn, the book writer, Ivan Menchell and myself were having lunch in La Jolla, San Diego, where the show was 'trying out' as they say. One of the producers walked in and said, 'Hi guys, great music, great lyrics,' and he then looked at the waiting book writer and said, 'Great shirt.'

PARODIES CAN BE FUN

It takes more talent to write music but it takes more courage to write lyrics. **Johnny Mercer**

I got to know the great lyric writer Sammy Cahn well over the years, although he didn't come to London often. He was terrified of flying, he said, 'I've made a deal with the birds, I don't fly and they don't write songs.' He was born in a poor and rough part of New York. When he won his Oscar for his song 'Call Me Irresponsible' he said in his acceptance speech, 'How about that? A five-syllable word from a kid who came from a one-syllable neighbourhood!'

Sammy was famous for his parodies of famous songs. They were brilliant but a little naughty. He wrote things like:

> You made me love you
> You woke me up to do it

And:

> The girl that I marry will have to be
> A nympho who owns a distillery

And my favourite:

> This is my first affair
> So what goes where?

PARODIES CAN BE FUN

A few years ago there was a big fund-raising dinner to celebrate the Jewish contribution to the arts, particularly in music and film. I compèred the star-studded evening and wrote a parody to the tune of 'Hava Nagilla'. If you know the tune please sing along:

> Streisand and Stephen Sondheim and Gustav Mahler
> Bob Dylan and Isaac Stern
> Stan Getz and Leonard Bernstein, the Gershwin Brothers
> Cy Coleman and Jerome Kern
> Berlin – Rodgers and Hart
> Jolson and Lionel Bart
> Amy Winehouse and Billy Joel
>
> Cantor and Frankie Vaughan
> Joel Grey and Goldie Hawn
> Andre Previn – no, not Nat King Cole!
> Topol and Bette Midler
> Kurt Weill and there's Michael Nyman
> Art Garfunkel and Paul Simon
> There's many more, many more
> She didn't look it but so was Dinah Shore
>
> Newley and Marvin Hamlisch, there's Neil Sedaka
> Let's not forget Jule Styne
> Heifitz and Carly Simon and Randy Newman
> Barry Manilow and Kevin Klein
> Who'd have thought Harry James?
> But so many changed their names

Izhak Pearlman never changed his
Herb Alpert – Mel Tormé
Philip Glass, Eydie Gorme
Herbert Kretzmer (he wrote Les Miz)
Korngold and Frank Loesser
Lerner and Loewe and Jerry Herman
Benny Goodman – Ethel Merman
All of them Jews
Talented Jews
Let's raise a glass to them tonight.

Many of the songwriters of the Great American Songbook were children of Jewish immigrants and the English language was something that had to be learned. The only exception to this was Cole Porter, who was born to a wealthy family in Indiana. All the others – apart from Alan Jay Lerner and Stephen Sondheim – came from humble beginnings. Cole Porter's lyrics were glossy and ritzy and reflected his lifestyle. He would summer in Antibes or Venice and would rub shoulders with High Society. Songs about swell parties and millionaires came easy to him. He would use words like camembert and Champagne in the depression years and somehow take away the drabness of the day. I love what Jule Styne said about him, 'Cole Porter has the brand of sophistication that can make a shopgirl know the 21 Club or El Morocco without ever having been there.'

Alan Jay Lerner has said that people in musical theatre frequently play the pointless game of comparisons. Was Ira Gershwin better than Cole

Porter? Was Oscar Hammerstein superior to Larry Hart? He has gone on to say that it's pointless because they were all master craftsmen, each with an expression of their own. Talking about Larry Hart he says, 'There is a tenderness in some of Larry's lyrics that always catches me off guard and brings a tear to my eye.' Listen to 'Bewitched, Bothered and Bewildered' and you'll see what I mean.

ROBBIE WILLIAMS – THE EARLY YEARS

My son Clive was working with Robbie and the record producer Trevor Horn in 2009. Some of the songs didn't make lyrical sense and Clive suggested to Robbie that I pop in to chat about them. I had an appointment to meet him at 3pm at Sarm Studios off the Portobello Road. Naturally I was early, but Robbie turned up at 4.30 saying he had overslept. He had had a sleepless night and took a pill at 7 a.m.

I was really surprised by his size. He is a big lad and extremely warm. He played me two songs that I don't think Stephen Hawking could have figured out what they were about. The third song, 'Morning Sun', was the best but it was still impossible to follow the story. He hugged me and kept apologising for keeping me waiting. We got to work and he was trying to justify the words he had written. I tried to explain that anyone listening to this song would not have a clue what it was about. He did explain to me that the first verse is about his religious teacher in school who kept on and on about Jesus. I said that would be fine if you mentioned the words 'teacher' and 'school'. We talked like this throughout our writing session. In between struggling to come up with the right words we got to know each other. We talked about Matt Monro, who he adored. Robbie's dad is Peter Conway, a comedian and singer who worked with Matt. We had a lot of laughs that day and he was eager to know how I worked with other composers. He was without doubt one of the most fragile stars I have ever met. He had no confidence. I kept telling him things to boost him up. Basically, all the fame and fortune hadn't done him any favours. I gave him my 'Keep your mind off your mind' speech, which really registered. I remember calling Shirley from the studio saying that he's a lovely boy and I hope he sorts himself out.

As a writer I am baffled by his words. There is nothing of the traditional songwriter about him. Most of the lines make no sense, except to him, and that's all he cares about. Maybe that's what makes him Robbie Williams. His lyrics don't follow any logic and it was challenging writing with him. Still, we finished the song, which became a single and did very well. We talked about writing some more together but at that time I knew it wouldn't be easy to follow his train of thought. He seemed confused and ill at ease with himself. It showed in his disjointed imagery. I remember him asking me about my long marriage to Shirley, 'How did you make it last?' I said that you both have to want the same things. I hadn't bumped into Robbie for many years until I wrote the song 'Hey Tiger' for the film *The Tiger Who Came to Tea*. Robbie sang the song. When he saw me he said he's never forgotten that line I said – You both have to want the same things. I was thrilled to see him looking as fit as a fiddle with a beautiful wife and three children. He gave me a copy of his latest album and I was shocked. I understood every word.

CLINGING TO THE WRECKAGE

The song is ended but the melody lingers on. **Irving Berlin**

The story goes that one day Cole Porter said in amazement to Rodgers and Hammerstein, 'You mean it took two of you to write one song?' I dread to think what Cole Porter would say today when it's commonplace for nine songwriters to walk on stage to collect an Ivor Novello Award. One or two or three of them may write what they call the top line, two, three or four of them may provide the 'beats' and the rest may throw in a word or two. The music business is unrecognisable compared to how it used to be. I recently met Noel Gallagher at a music business function and he asked me what instrument I played. I told him I didn't play any instrument. He then said well how did you write 'Diamonds Are Forever'? I said John Barry sent me the tune and I put words to it. He went pale and said loudly, 'No fucking way!' I said that's how it always used to be and I said when I write with Van Morrison I give him some words and he puts a tune to them. Again, only this time a little louder, 'No fucking way!' I asked him how he wrote his songs and he said he spends forever getting the track right and when he's happy with it he tries to come up with some words. It isn't my style but I felt like screaming, 'No fucking way!'

Noel wrote a fascinating article for a music paper saying in his opinion 'co-writing is the death of art'. He cites that *Music Week*'s research revealed that an average of 5.34 writers worked on last year's top one hundred singles. He mentions some songs that have twenty or thirty writers and as he eloquently puts it, 'It's all this major record label shit.' His main gripe is that if there are so many people contributing to a song no true artists are created, only people who dabble in song writing a bit.

I couldn't agree with him more. Can you imagine the likes of Rubens or Renoir or Van Gogh saying to each other, 'You do the sky, I'll do the trees and the moon and you do the daffodils.' *Didn't Rubens's studio?*

The seismic shift began with the Beatles. They started writing their own songs and, before you could say 'Strawberry Fields Forever', everyone seemed to follow suit. If you look at today's top hundred songs on the hit parade you will see that practically every single one was written by the artist or producer. The professional songwriter is redundant.

Unless you write with the singer or the producer there is little chance of your song being recorded. If you are not a performer yourself and you don't know performers or record producers you may as well forget it.

When I wrote 'Born Free' in the sixties around six hundred people recorded the song. When 'Skyfall' won the Oscar I don't think anyone recorded it apart from Adele. No one covers songs any more which means it's harder than ever to write a standard these days. All those talented writers like Mike D'abo ('Build Me Up Buttercup'), Greenaway and Cook ('You've Got Your Troubles'), Richard Kerr ('Mandy') and hundreds more all over the world have nowhere to sell their wares. When we meet the phrase 'clinging to the wreckage' comes up a lot.

I was very lucky in pursuing a career in musical theatre and films. When you write for the stage you get a percentage of the box office so if the show is successful you can do very well. If the show isn't successful you've spent a few years of your life on a project and earned zilch. Jerry Herman, the man who wrote *Hello Dolly!* and *Mame* put it accurately when he said, 'There's no money in the theatre but if you get a hit there's rivers of money.'

Apart from a very few radio stations no one plays the old songs any more. This means that your old hits become diminishing assets. This, coupled with the fact that no one is recording your new works, makes you feel that the professional songwriter will soon be as rare as the bald-headed eagle. Some of my film songs, like 'Diamonds Are Forever' and 'Born Free', are often on television and that perpetuates the life of a song.

When Irving Berlin was in a pessimistic mood about the state of the music business he wrote a poem about the brief life of a popular song. It's a long poem so here's just the last part:

> Popular song, you will never be missed
> Once your composer has ceased to exist
> While Chopin, Verdi, Beethoven and Liszt
> Live on with each generation
> Still, though you die after having your sway
> To be forgotten the very next day
> A rose lives and dies the very same way
> Let that be your consolation

Every now and then that old chestnut of a phrase 'songs are coming back' echoes through the corridors of the music industry. It only takes one song with a hint of a melody and a few intelligent words and older producers and writers start salivating, expecting a flood of quality standards to rival the golden age of quality songwriters.

This period varies depending on your age.

The great artistes of my generation such as Sinatra, Streisand, Tony Bennett, Nat King Cole, Judy Garland, Dean Martin, Ella Fitzgerald, Sammy Davis Jr, all had one thing in common – they didn't write songs. They sang songs written by the best song-writers in the world and our ears, hearts and lives were all the better for it.

CONNIE FRANCIS

I got to know the singer Connie Francis when she came over here and we've always stayed in touch. Connie became a huge recording artiste all over the world, her biggest hits being 'Who's Sorry Now?' and 'Stupid Cupid'. It was a glittering career and then on 8 November 1974 a tragedy occurred. She was raped at the Howard Johnson Lodge in Jericho, New York. She subsequently sued the motel chain for failing to provide adequate security and reportedly won a $2.5 million settlement. After that terrible incident Connie went into depression and didn't sing for four years.

In her autobiography she says that she heard a song of mine on the radio, sung by Shirley Bassey, and it helped her to get back on her feet. From that moment she began taking singing lessons to get her voice back in shape. Since then she hasn't stopped working, mainly concert appearances all over the world.

The song she is referring to is 'If I Never Sing Another Song'. The music is by the Austrian composer Udo Jürgens, who incidentally wrote the music to 'Walk Away'. The lyric tells the story of someone who was a major star many years ago but is uncertain of what the future holds. It has been sung by many singers, usually as their closing number. Matt Monro sang it first; some of the other versions are by Sammy Davis Jr, Johnny Ray, Frankie Laine and of course Connie Francis.

CONNIE FRANCIS

'If I Never Sing Another Song'

In my heyday,

Young girls wrote to me

Everybody seemed to have time

To devote to me

Everyone I saw all swore they knew me

Once upon a song

Main attraction, couldn't buy a seat

The celebrity celebrities would die to meet

I've had every accolade bestowed on me

And so you see

If I never sing another song

It wouldn't bother me

I've had my share of fame

You know my name

If I never sing another song

Or take another bow

I would get by

But I'm not sure how

Always posing but you love it all

Though you have to learn to act

Like you're above it all

Above it all

Everything I did the world applauded

Once upon a star

Framed citations

THE SANEST GUY IN THE ROOM

Hang on every wall
Got a scrapbook full of quotes
I can't recall at all
There were times
I thought the world belonged to me
And so you see

If I never sing another song
It shouldn't bother me
I've had my share of fame
You know my name
If I never sing another song
Or take another bow
I would get by
But I'm not sure how

NASHVILLE

After writing so much about my love for beautifully crafted songs, you may be surprised to hear that I love country music! It ignores the rules laid down by the Berlins and Porters but it doesn't bother me. The lyrics aren't immaculate and the melodies are rarely tuneful. There is an old saying about what it takes to write a country song – 'Three chords and the truth'. All great country songs are lyric-led. You have to find a way of saying something in a different way, usually about cheating, loss, heartbreak, gambling, family or faith.

I went to Nashville once in the eighties and wrote about a dozen songs, most of them in one day. All the writers there, and there are hundreds, are on red alert when it comes to finding an idea for a song. You only have to say to someone, 'Good to see you' and they come back at you with, 'Hey, what a great title.'

I stayed at a hotel called the Spence Manor which had a swimming pool shaped like a guitar. My publisher sent me there to work with some up-and-coming writers. It was an adrenaline rush kind of trip. All my collaborators played great guitar and were great singers. Also, they often write four or five songs a day. Tim Rice often speaks of how much easier it is to come up with the tunes than it is the lyrics. I couldn't agree more. Once the composer comes up with a verse and chorus they are usually repeated and his work is done. The sweaty-palmed lyric writer has to concoct a story that has a beginning, middle and end. In Nashville, you don't have time to walk around parks or sleep on an idea. You have to think on your feet, and even if you come up with drivel, these guys make every song sound like a smash.

The British writer Tony Hiller, who wrote 'Save Your Kisses for Me', went to Nashville every year for about twenty years. He told me he had written about two hundred songs there but only a very few were recorded. The competition is scary. He became well known out there, and at those SODS dinners I used to introduce him as 'The Rhinestone Rabbi'.

As well as those heart-wrenching songs, I love the humour in some country titles:

'If You Wanna Keep Your Beer Cold (Put it Next to Her Heart)'
'How Can I Miss You If You Won't Go Away?'
'You Can't Have Your Kate and Edith'

And my favourite:

'I've Never Been to Bed with an Ugly Woman (But I've Sure Woken Up with a Few)'

Nashville is probably the only place in the world where the singer or producer doesn't insist on being a co-writer. Carrie Underwood, Dolly Parton, Reba McEntire, Garth Brooks, Brad Paisley are all smart enough to know that the song is the most important thing and are open about where it comes from.

THANK YOU FOR ENDING YOUR WEEK WITH ME

For just over seven years I have been presenting my own show on BBC's Radio Two. I took over from the legendary broadcaster David Jacobs. David heard a show I did when Elaine Paige was on holiday and I stood in for her. He recommended me to take over from him in his 11 p.m. slot every Sunday. This has been one of the most joyful of jobs I have ever done. I play mostly the Great American Songbook, which includes all the great writers from my generation. I also talk about the stories behind the songs which the listeners seem to enjoy as much as the music. I've met a lot of the writers and singers that I play so there is always a large dollop of name-dropping in every show. These anecdotes are the introductions to the records I play.

As regular listeners will know I lost my precious wife Shirley on 7 March. I don't mind telling you that every song I play has a deeper significance since then. Your compassionate letters have helped me enormously and so many people have bombarded me with offers of dinners and well wishes. I try my hardest

207

not to get too sentimental, but when you come across a song like 'I'll Only Miss Her When I Think of Her', sung by Frank Sinatra, it's pretty impossible.

| MOVIE SONGS

For a brief spell when I left Denmark Street I went to work for a company called Film Music. It was owned by the Rank Organisation and had fancy offices off Bond Street. The company was run by a delightful man called Harold Shampan, and he gave me my first stab at writing a song for a film. It was called *Very Important Person* and starred James Robertson Justice and Eric Sykes. Leslie Phillips played the part of an RAF man in the Second World War who had the catchphrase 'Tickety-boo'. The director Ken Annakin thought it would be a good idea if he had a little song called 'Tickety-boo'. Leslie sings the following while he is having a bath.

> When you think it's going to be one of those days
> When no lucky star is high above you
> Then you better hang on to this simple phrase
> And everyone will say I love you
> Tickety-boo, Tickety-boo, Tickety-boo.

Those few words were my introduction to the silver screen. Maybe I peaked too early. Here is a list of some of the obscure oddities I've written for the screen and some that were a gift.

The Long Duel

This film starred Yul Brynner and Trevor Howard. The tagline for the film was: 'The blazing passions of a land, it's proud warriors . . . it's exotic women . . . bursting aflame in revolt . . . fought out in the Himalayas and across the scorching plains of India.' The director was Ken Annakin again, the man who gave me my first cinematic break with *Very Important Person*. He wanted me to write a song about the futility of war for the end-titles. I got together with the composer John Scott and we came up with 'When the World Is Ready'. It was sung by Vince Hill.

Pancho Villa

This film starred Telly Savalas, and was a kind of Spaghetti Western. I was asked to write a philosophical song about life. The composer was John Cacavas who I got to know on one of my many trips to Los Angeles. The song we wrote was called 'We All End Up the Same' and it was sung in the film by Telly himself. If you're ever up at 3am switch on the television and you could come across it.

The Midas Run

I was delighted when I got a call from Elmer Bernstein to write a song for this film because it starred Fred Astaire. I was brought down to earth with a bump when I learned he was playing the part of a secret agent and he wouldn't be singing or dancing. Hey ho! We wrote a song called 'The Midas Run' because that's what you did in those days.

The Dove

This was a delightful film and a true story about a boy who sails around the world in a 23-foot sloop. On his journey he falls in love. My memory of that film is that it was produced by Gregory Peck and I met him with John Barry at one of the recording sessions. He was even more handsome in the flesh than he was on screen. The song John and I wrote was 'Sail the Summer Winds' and it was sung by Lyn Paul who used to be part of The New Seekers. John was always fond of the song and if you have a moment you can find it on YouTube.

The Bitch

I wrote a few songs for this film starring Joan Collins. The music was by Biddu, the man who wrote 'Kung Fu Fighting'. The title song was recorded by The Olympic Runners and was a hit single and the soundtrack album was also a hit. The film was panned by the critics and banned from the BBC but was nevertheless a commercial success.

The Party

I have treasured memories of working on this film with Henry Mancini. It was directed by Blake Edwards and starred Peter Sellers. The story is about a bungling actor (portrayed by Sellers) who makes terrible social mistakes. He comes from India and is accidentally invited to a lavish Hollywood dinner party but is embarrassingly ignorant of Western ways.

The film is now considered a classic comedy cult film. I find it hilarious and it's many people's favourite film. Henry and I had to write a romantic song to be sung at the party by Claudine Longet.

While she is singing it, Sellers is doing some zany comedy behind her. This ruins the song of which we were so proud. The song was called 'Nothing to Lose' and was often referred to by Blake Edwards, and his wife Julie Andrews, as their song. It has been recorded by Vic Damone and Matt Monro.

The Pink Panther Strikes Again

This was my second collaboration with Henry Mancini and Blake Edwards. It was also my second movie song sung by Tom Jones, the first being 'Thunderball'.

This song was called 'Come to Me' and it was nominated for an Oscar. Tom sang the song at the Awards ceremony. The film starred Peter Sellers as Chief Inspector Jacques Clouseau and he was at the top of his game. Writing with Henry, or Hank as we call him, was a dream. Not only did he write wonderful melodies, but he also knew all the best restaurants in London and Los Angeles.

Work Is a Four-Letter Word

This was a strange film. It starred the respected British actor David Warner and Cilla Black in her first, and I think only, lead role in a film. It was directed by the legendary theatre director Peter Hall. The film was pretty difficult to follow; all I remember of it is David Warner trying to grow mushrooms in his house. Cilla recorded the title song, but it was later covered by the lauded and influential band The Smiths. When I tell people that The Smiths recorded a song of mine they look at me in a different light.

Gulliver's Travels

I wrote the screenplay as well as the lyrics for this film starring that loveable hellraiser Richard Harris. I had many meetings in his gothic house in Holland Park, now owned by Led Zeppelin guitarist Jimmy Page.

Apart from Richard, the whole film was animated. I wrote the score with John Barry. However the Belgian producer wasn't fond of it and replaced John with Michel Legrand. It must have been a terrible chore for Michel – he had to write new tunes to a film that was already shot, so the synching of the animated characters must have been a nightmare. I also think it was a mistake as John's music was far more tuneful.

> Sometimes it takes a long time for a song to see the light of day. In 1932, Rodgers and Hart wrote a song called 'Prayer' for the MGM film *Hollywood Party* starring Jean Harlow. At the last minute, Jean decided not to do the picture and the song was dropped. Larry Hart wrote new lyrics to the same tune and it was supposed to go into the film *Manhattan Melodrama* – that time the song was called 'The Bad In Every Man'. It was also cut from the film. Jack Robbins, who was working for Paramount around that time, always loved the melody and suggested that Larry should write a commercial lyric to it. It proved to be third time lucky. Larry called it 'Blue Moon'.

Gold

This film starred Roger Moore and has a bit of a cult following. I wrote three songs for it with the magnificent Elmer Bernstein. One of them was 'Wherever Love Takes Me', which was nominated for an Oscar. It was up against 'Blazing Saddles' by Mel Brooks and 'Little Prince' by Lerner and Loewe. We didn't stand a chance because the biggest film of that year was *The Towering Inferno* and it was the song from that, 'We May Never Love Like This Again', that won the coveted prize. Honestly, some things are so unfair!

Dances with Wolves

This was an American epic Western film starring, produced and directed by Kevin Costner. Many people consider this to be John Barry's best score and he justifiably won the Oscar for it. The main theme was beautiful, and John asked me to put words to it. I asked him what it should be about and he gave me a one-word brief – 'heroes'. I then wrote 'Here's to the Heroes' and John thought it was one of my best songs. It is often used whenever there are military gatherings to honour soldiers, sailors or airmen.

Here's to the heroes

Those few who dare

Heading for glory

Living a prayer

Here's to the heroes

Who change our lives

Thanks to the heroes

Freedom survives

Here's to the heroes

Who never rest

They are the chosen

We are the blessed

Here's to the heroes

> Who aim so high
> Here's to the heroes
> Who do or die

Out of Africa

John Barry won another Oscar for the music to this wonderful film starring Meryl Streep and Robert Redford. Once again he asked me to write words to the haunting main theme. I called it 'Places' (John liked simple titles) and Aled Jones made a fine record of it.

A Walk in the Spring Rain

I was so excited to get this assignment because the title was beautiful and perfect for a romantic song. Not only that, it starred Ingrid Bergman and Anthony Quinn. The music was by my old collaborator Elmer Bernstein and the song was sung by a highly respected singer called Michael Dees. Unfortunately, the film was seen by about four people and what looked so promising just fizzled away. In this highly digitalised world it's nice to know that you can still find these songs on Spotify or YouTube.

Boom!

This was another film with a glittering cast: Elizabeth Taylor, Richard Burton and Noël Coward. With all that star power it was still a critical disaster. *Newsweek* called it, 'A pointless, pompous nightmare.' However I did enjoy writing a song for it with Johnny Dankworth. It was called 'Hideaway' and was sung in the film by Georgie Fame.

I'll Never Forget What's 'Isname

I must say I do miss having Michael Winner as a neighbour. We lived opposite each other for over twenty years. He was larger than life and the street is not the same without him. When he died in 2013, I had a call from his wife Geraldine asking me if I knew the Jewish prayer for the dead and could I speak it in Hebrew. I said, unfortunately yes. She asked me if I would say it at Michael's funeral at Willesden cemetery. Obviously it's a solemn prayer called kaddish and it seemed bizarre to say this with Michael Parkinson and Madeleine Lloyd Webber either side of me. I do not wear my Jewishness on my sleeve so they were shocked by my Hebraic skills.

Michael directed this film which starred Orson Welles and Oliver Reed. It received mostly positive reviews and it gave me the chance to work with the French composer Frances Lai. Frances had enormous success writing the scores for *A Man and a Woman* and *Love Story*. Our song was called *One Day Soon* and was recorded by Matt Monro and Tom Jones.

Cahill US Marshall

This was my second John Wayne film, the first being *True Grit*. This film comes up a lot on television. Once again I worked with Elmer Bernstein. We wrote a reflective song sung around a camp-fire called 'A Man Gets to Thinkin''. The film was not considered a Western classic but still took over $3 million at the box office.

Alice's Adventures in Wonderland

This was a truly star-studded film led by Michael Crawford, Peter Sellers, Dudley Moore, Spike Milligan, Flora Robson,

Ralph Richards and with Robert Helpmann as the Mad Hatter. It was a full-blown musical and John Barry was the composer once again. The film had a royal première and I stood in line to be introduced to the Queen. It was a great moment, much better than the one when, during the film, I leaned across to see Her Majesty was sleeping!

Svengali

This was a film made for television and it starred Peter O'Toole and Jodie Foster. I was amazed how well Jodie sang. John Barry and I wrote a few songs for her and I often get letters asking how you can get hold of them. Well for some I have a cassette copy only, and I would not let it out of my sight. But there are two that you can get on the usual streaming outlets – they are 'Getting Some Feeling Back in My Heart' and 'One Dream at a Time'. The film wasn't received too well; in fact, one acerbic critic wrote, '*Svengali* is an excellent example of how a truly brilliant actor can make unwatchable material quite enjoyable at times.'

Hoffman

I loved working with the late Australian composer Ron Grainer. He is known mostly for writing the scores to *Doctor Who*, *The Prisoner*, *Steptoe and Son* and *Tales of the Unexpected*. He wasn't known as a songwriter and our brief was to write a romantic song for Matt Monro to sing. We came up with 'If There Ever Is a Next Time' and it was one of Matt's personal favourites. The film was a strange one, and once again starred Peter Sellers. Only this time he was playing a straight role – no laughs. Peter wasn't happy with the film and offered to buy it back from the production company.

The director Alvin Rakoff said, 'He couldn't rely on mimicry, and he went through the torture of not knowing who Hoffman was because he didn't know who he was.'

The Vengeance of Fu Man Chu

This was a typically melodramatic film starring Christopher Lee. The music was by Malcolm Lockyer. Malcolm was a highly respected composer and conductor who died aged 52 in 1976. I don't think he had ever written a song before but he came up with two cracking melodies for the two songs we were commissioned to write. They were 'Where Are the Men' and 'The Real Me'. Both songs were sung in the film by Samantha Jones. The film has a bit of a cult following – recently Michael Ball came up to me all excited and said, 'I didn't know you did *The Vengeance of Fu Man Chu*, I bloody love that film!'

Mary, Queen of Scots

Another collaboration with John Barry and an opportunity to put words to his main theme. The film starred Vanessa Redgrave and Glenda Jackson. The song we wrote was 'This Way Mary' and there were two beautiful recordings by Johnny Mathis and Matt Monro.

Walkabout

This film was directed by Nicolas Roeg and is considered to be one of his masterpieces, along with *Don't Look Now* and *The Man Who Fell to Earth*. John Barry, yet again, wrote the music and I put words to the main theme. One of John's favourite singers was Tony Bennett and he was delighted, as was I, when Tony recorded it.

Hollywood party with Michael Jackson, Sophia Loren and Petula Clark. *(author's collection)*

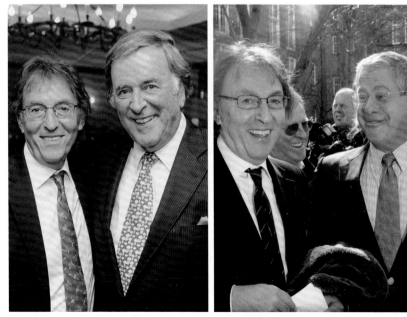

Terry Wogan, my much missed broadcasting hero. *(author's collection)*

With the ever-jovial Sir Cameron Mackintosh. *(Alan Davidson/Shutterstock)*

A SODS dinner with Tim Rice and Lionel Bart. *(author's collection)*

Me and my snooker table. *(author's collection)*

Me with my snooker hero Jimmy White. *(author's collection)*

With Elmer Bernstein. Happier days before we opened *Merlin* on Broadway. *(author's collection)*

Three theatrical titans: Liza Minnelli *(top)*, Alan Jay Lerner *(above)* and Jule Styne *(left)*. *(author's collection)*

Me with Charles Aznavour. *(author's collection)*

Michael Ball and Ann Crumb in *Aspects of Love*.
(Donald Cooper/Photostage)

With Barbra Streisand and
Christopher Hampton.
(author's collection)

Marti Webb in *Tell Me
on a Sunday*. *(Donald
Cooper/Photostage)*

Sir George Martin presenting me with a special Ivor Novello Fellowship award. *(author's collection)*

Me with my brother Michael. *(author's collection)*

Me receiving my Songwriters Hall of Fame Award in New York. *(author's collection)*

Receiving the fellowship from Paul McCartney at the Liverpool Institute for Performing Arts. *(author's collection)*

(*above*) Marvin Hamlisch, Shirley and me at the opening of *The Goodbye Girl*. *(author's collection)*

(*left*) A. R. Rahman, John Barry and me. *(author's collection)*

With Quincy Jones. *(author's collection)*

With Tony Bennett and Van Morrison. *(author's collection)*

Receiving my OBE.
(author's collection)

Me with my siblings: Adele, Cyril, Nita and Michael.
(author's collection)

Happy days: me with Grant, Shirley and Clive.
(author's collection)

Me and Shirley. *(author's collection)*

The Tamarind Seed

Another John Barry collaboration! The film starred Julie Andrews and Omar Sharif. It was a romantic drama written and directed by Julie's husband Blake Edwards. John wrote a haunting theme which I called 'Play it Again'. It was sung by Wilma Reading. If you have the time have a listen to it on the net.

Tom's Midnight Garden

This was based on the famous children's fantasy novel and is regarded as a classic. It was the start of many collaborations with the gifted composer Debbie Wiseman. The song that brought us together was called 'After Always' and was sung in the film by Barbara Dickson.

I don't want to list every song I've written for films because the films and/or the songs aren't worthy. But here are a few more:

Isadora – Maurice Jarre

Where's Jack? – Elmer Bernstein

Doc Savage: The Man of Bronze – John Philip Sousa

Mayerling – Francis Lai

First Love – Mark London

House of a Thousand Dolls – Mark London

The Southern Star – George Garvarentz

Sinful Davey – Ken Thorne

Hot Millions – Laurie Johnson

Mr Jericho – George Martin

Run Wild, Run Free – David Whitaker

The Last Valley – John Barry

THE SANEST GUY IN THE ROOM

The Golden Seal – John Barry

Walking Tall – Walter Scharf

A Doll's House – John Barry

Golden Needles – Lalo Schifrin

Private Eye – John Barry

Paul and Michelle – Michel Colombier

The Return of Maxwell Smart (also known as *The Nude Bomb*)
– Lalo Schifrin

The Worst Witch – Charles Strouse

Love Among the Ruins – John Barry

AMIGOS PARA SIEMPRE

In 1992, Andrew Lloyd Webber was asked to write the theme for the Summer Olympics in Barcelona. He asked me to do the lyric but I was told it had to be called 'Amigos para Siempre' ('Friends for Life'). It was decided that it would be sung by Sarah Brightman and José Carreras. I found José to be a delightful man and very funny. When I first met him he said to me, 'I've never met a living lyricist before.' Like many opera singers, he likes to sing popular songs. I've always felt uneasy about this because their accents are so strong and the lyric rarely comes out how you want it to. In musicals it's the words that carry the story and there are many hit musicals that have inferior music. I find it impossible to be moved when an opera singer sings a Richard Rodgers song. In fact when Richard Rodgers used to audition people with trained voices he would say, 'Now sing it as though you never had a singing lesson.'

> I don't have to say a word to you
> You seem to know
> Whatever mood I'm going through
> Feel as though I've known you forever
> You can look into my eyes and see
> The way I feel

THE SANEST GUY IN THE ROOM

And how the world is treating me

Maybe I have known you forever

Amigos para siempre

Means you'll always be my friend

Amics per sempre

Means a love that cannot end

Friends for life

Not just a summer or a spring

Amigos para siempre

I feel you near me

Even when we are apart

Just knowing you are in this world

Can warm my heart

Friends for life

Not just a summer or a spring

Amigos para siempre

We share memories

I won't forget

And we'll share more my friend

We haven't started yet

Something happens when we're together

When I look at you

I wonder why

There has to come a time

When we must say goodbye

I'm alive when we are together

AMIGOS PARA SIEMPRE

Amigos para siempre
Means you'll always be my friend
Amics per sempre
Means a love that cannot end
Friends for life
Not just a summer or a spring
Amigos para siempre

I feel you near me
Even when we are apart
Just knowing you are in this world
Can warm my heart
Friends for life
Not just a summer or a spring
Amigos para siempre
When I look at you
I wonder why
There has to come a time
When we must say goodbye
I'm alive when we are together

Amigos para siempre
Means you'll always be my friend
Amics per sempre
Means a love that cannot end
Friends for life
Not just a summer or a spring
Amigos para siempre

The great Richard Rodgers had a reputation for being stiff and formal and hard to get to know, but I came across an interview he did and found him to be very amusing. He was talking about his father who was a doctor and he said his father loved classical music, in fact he found all doctors loved classical music. He went on to say that the best place in the world to have a heart attack would be at a Royal Philharmonic concert because there was bound to be a doctor in the same row as you!

CAN ANYONE WRITE A MUSICAL?

In 1984, the Performing Rights Society financed an annual competition to encourage writers to write for musical theatre. It became well known as The Vivian Ellis Prize. I was the chairman and host of the prize for fifteen years. Vivian Ellis was the distinguished composer of 'Bless the Bride' and the song 'Spread a Little Happiness'. He was a snobbish, condescending and mean-spirited sort of man, but very funny. He went everywhere with his loyal sister Hermione. They lived together close to Holland Park and I used to see them often sitting on the same bench. I once asked him why he always sat in the same place and he said, 'It's one of my greatest pleasures to sit here and listen to the people misidentify the flowers.' When he was ill I called him in hospital to ask how he was and he said, 'On top of the world. The sun is shining, I've had a good breakfast, and I've just read a dreadful review of Sondheim's new musical.'

The Vivian Ellis Prize took place at the Guildhall School of Music and the judges, including Andrew Lloyd Webber, Cameron Mackintosh and Vivian himself, were hoping to find the next Cole Porters and Irving Berlins, but all we found were Irving Porters. There is a misconception that the world is populated with budding musical-theatre geniuses. Year after year we waded through the same predictable subjects. The ones that came up the

225

most were 'The Story of Dorian Grey', 'Rasputin' and 'The Hunchback of Notre Dame'.

It was difficult not to be rude about some of the entries; one longed to tell the writers not to leave their jobs and if they had left to try and get it back. In the sixteen years the Prize ran, it produced only two glowing successes. One was the lyricist Charles Hart. He entered a musical based on Moll Flanders – it wasn't particularly noteworthy but the lyrics were impressive. Andrew spotted this and asked him to write the lyrics to *The Phantom of the Opera*. I collaborated with him later on *Aspects of Love*. The other success was the team of George Styles and Anthony Drewe, who shone with their entry based on Rudyard Kipling's *Just So* stories. They have since written many musicals and Cameron has sort of taken them under his wing by asking them to write additional songs for *Mary Poppins* and *Half a Sixpence*.

Andrew has said on many occasions that it's time for a new Lloyd Webber/Tim Rice team to emerge. This hasn't happened in this country. However, in America we have seen quite a few major talents score big in the theatre. Lin-Manuel Miranda was a gamechanger with his inventive musical *Hamilton*.

Benj Pasek and Justin Paul have scored big with their two film musicals *La La Land* and *The Greatest Showman* as well as their Broadway smash *Dear Evan Hansen*.

There are no set rules for how to write a musical and there is certainly no magic formula. It is probably the most collaborative art form, where stress and elation are strange bedfellows.

Bette Davis once famously said, 'Growing old ain't for cissies.' The same could be said for writing musicals.

CAN ANYONE WRITE A SONG?

Writing a song is very different to writing a musical. You can write about anything, there is no scenario to restrict you and, as opposed to the songs I was brought up with, the craft used by the greats can be ignored today. I do think anyone can write a song but not necessarily a great one.

An old friend of mine is Arthur Hamilton who wrote the standards 'Cry Me a River' and 'I Can Sing a Rainbow'. I have seen him give a lecture that made so much sense I will share some of it here. He said that the qualities required to become a successful songwriter are the same to become a successful anything: talent, focus, relentless ambition, patience, pride and luck. As for advice or tips or special warm-up techniques he suggests that all young writers study the structure and content of the greatest songs of the last century: Jerome Kern, Rodgers and Hart, George and Ira Gershwin and Oscar Hammerstein. There was never a word in them that didn't matter and never a note that didn't have a reason for being that particular note. After digesting their material every young writer should allow his or her voice to emerge. The world is waiting to hear your song, not your idea of how Cole Porter would write one today. And as for warm-up techniques, I don't think we are ever not warming up.

Some of today's songwriters are brilliant and have found their 'own voice' as Arthur suggests. Ed Sheeran is a standout and so are Max Martin, Billie Eilish and Tom Odell.

> I met Mickey Rooney once when he was over here and I told him that I liked a song he wrote called 'Spoken For' which Sammy Davis Jr recorded. He was over the moon that I knew it as he hadn't written many songs. He told me he loved writing songs more than anything else. He was very funny off stage. He was married eight times and when he was asked by a reporter why he never married Rita Hayworth, he said 'Didn't I?'

SHIRLEY, YOU DON'T HAVE TO MAKE THE BED

If you got air miles every time you ordered from Deliveroo I'd have enough to get me to Jupiter. First I only managed to make boiled eggs and now I can make sardines on toast all by myself. There is no evidence in the house that Shirley isn't here. Nothing has been changed and I like it this way. I open her wardrobe and I can still smell her tuberose perfume. I look at the book on her bedside table which is the last book she read – *Eleanor Oliphant Is Completely Fine*. She loved that book. I asked her if I would like it; she said, 'You would, but you won't finish it.' It has always been a habit of mine not to finish books. Once I feel I've got the plot and the writing style I usually switch back to my poetry books. I've always felt that poetry says twice as much as prose in half the time. I used to read poems to Shirley in bed before she went to sleep. They were usually by American poets like Edna St.Vincent Millay or Emily Dickinson; occasionally I'd read her funny ones by Pam Ayres which always brought a smile to her face.

When it came to Shirley's birthday it was incredibly difficult to find her a present. Many times I pleaded with her to let me buy her a diamond ring or a Prada dress. She would say, 'What do I need that for?' Neither of us were impressed by expensive trappings. When people ask me what car do I drive I say, 'A blue one.'

Shirley was also very happy to do the housework with our cleaner! The house was always spotless and she enjoyed doing the most menial jobs – making the beds, ironing, hoovering. I couldn't talk her out of this. I said thankfully we can afford for you to do nothing in the house. She finally agreed for my shirts to be laundered. I have a wonderful cleaner but I now realise that without Shirley helping her it is beginning to look dustier than it's ever been. Just one of the telling signs that a home needs a woman's touch.

Shirley believed in prayer and every single night – no matter how late it was – she would close her eyes in bed and say, 'If you've got anything to say, say it now because I'm about to say my prayers.' If I did interrupt her she wouldn't answer till she finished them. Shirley always took a good five or six minutes to complete this ritual. She obviously included everyone she knew in them. I used to say to her, 'Can't you just say, "Bless them all" and leave it at that?'

I've been overwhelmed by the onslaught of kindness from friends. I have forced myself to go out to dinners and see shows because I know that's what she would want. I've heard of men who lose their partners and they never leave the house, just stay at home and drink. This has never entered my mind because Shirley would be furious with me. My son Grant said soon after she died, 'If I get dressed in the morning it's a result.'

I recently finished writing a song with David Arnold for a television version of the children's classic *The Tiger Who Came to Tea*. Shirley heard every song first before it went out into the world, and her not sitting in front of me with her eyes closed as she hung on every word is something that I will never get used to.

Nica Burns is a theatre owner and when I had lunch with her recently she asked me how I was doing. I was honest and said I miss the little things most: her telling me I should have put on the blue shirt, not telling her how beautiful she was, putting her necklace on because she could never find the clasp, watching the *Antiques Road Show* together. But most of all, I told Nica, there is no one to buy flowers for. The next day the most beautiful orchids arrived from her with a note saying, 'Shirley would want you to have flowers.'

THE TIGER WHO CAME TO TEA

The song for *The Tiger Who Came to Tea* came about after a phone call from David Arnold. He said he'd been asked to write the music for a television film based on Judith Kerr's multi-million-selling children's book. I said I've heard of it but what's it about. He said I should get a copy of it. I popped over the road to Waterstones, came back and read it in about five minutes. I called David back and said, 'It's the shortest book I've read since Jewish Astronauts.' He said yes but it's delightful and I've written a tune for it. He also warned me that Judith Kerr, although in her nineties, is very much involved and has to approve everything. Eventually we wrote the song and we waited anxiously for Judith's reaction. She was very happy but had a few quibbles. She thought the line 'Today won't come around again' was a bit too abstract. I had also written the lines:

We could listen to a big brass band
Or smell the onions from the hot dog stand

She called again saying she'd changed her mind about 'Today won't come around again' but she thought hot dog stand sounded 'too American and didn't fit with the very British feel of the book'. I changed the line to 'Or pick a flavour from the ice-cream van.'

This was a dream project and I'm only sorry I never got to meet Judith, who died before the film was completed.

'The Tiger Who Came to Tea'

Hey Tiger,
Glad you called c'mon in
There's lots of biscuits in the biscuit tin
Put on your smile and let the day begin
Today won't come around again
We got no rush
And we got nothin' planned
We can listen to a big brass band
Or pick a flavour from the ice-cream van
Today won't come around again

Hey Tiger,
When you see your chance go out and grab it
Be more like a tiger than a rabbit
You can make your spirits soar
By simply opening the door
Let's face it that's what doors are for
Tiger
Do the things you love while you are able
Time to get up from the kitchen table
Go ahead and open up the door

We can row a boat across the lake
And find a place that sells chocolate cake

THE SANEST GUY IN THE ROOM

All we have to do is stay awake!
Today won't come around again

Hey Tiger
When you see your chance go out and grab it
Be more like a tiger than a rabbit
You can make your spirits soar
By simply opening the door
Let's face it that's what doors are for
Tiger
Do the things you love while you are able
Time to get up from the kitchen table
Go ahead and open up the door

Hey Tiger
Glad you called c'mon in
There's lots of biscuits in the biscuit tin
Put on your smile and let the day begin
Today won't come around again
Today won't come around again
Today won't come around again

MORE LYRICISTS

The lyricist Leo Robin was most famous for his modesty. Whenever he wrote a successful song he said it was due to the genius of his collaborator, or the song was performed by a brilliant talent, or he 'got lucky'. Well Leo got lucky with 'Thanks for the Memory', 'Diamonds Are a Girl's Best Friend', 'Love Is Just Around the Corner' and many more. But Leo's luck ran out one day when Jule Styne asked him if he'd like to write the lyrics to a new show called *Funny Girl*. He read the script and said, 'This story's been done a thousand times, who wants to hear about a girl from the ghetto who turns out to be a big star?' So Leo Robin turned it down and the man who ended up writing the words was Bob Merrill. Leo must have felt sick every time he heard 'People' or 'Don't Rain on My Parade'.

The lyricist Irving Caesar was a great character. He said he wrote 'Swanee' with George Gershwin in ten minutes. He also said, 'I may write lousy but always fast.' One night he had a call from the composer Vincent Youmans who was excited about a melody he'd come up with. 'Not now,' he said, 'I'm half asleep.' Vincent wouldn't leave it at that, he kept playing him the melody over the phone. 'Okay,' said Irving, 'I'll give you a dummy lyric and I'll write you a proper one tomorrow. Picture you upon my knee, with tea for two and two for tea and me for you and you for

235

me alone.' Vincent loved it and said, 'keep going'. Irving did keep going and said he finished it in eight minutes! It may have been fast but it wasn't lousy.

VAN MORRISON

Van has a reputation of being ferociously grumpy and mean-spirited. I only know of this reputation because a lot of people have told me about it. Having gotten to know him these past few years I completely disagree with that assessment. When you first meet him he does have a look of a man who has just learned his flight has been delayed. But when you get him into talking about music or philosophy he can laugh like a member of a Jimmy Carr audience.

We met at a BMI dinner – a music-industry function that rewards songwriters annually by giving them certificates for their successes. They always announce previous winners of their Icon Award and Ray Davies, Tim Rice, Van and me were huddled together for photographs. He told me that he listens to my programme and we should meet for lunch. We have met regularly since then and we always end up talking about the great songwriters I play on my show. He is absolutely besotted by the Cole Porters and Irving Berlins of this world. I knew his big songs like 'Brown Eyed Girl' and 'Moondance' and a few others but I've never seen him live. He invited me to a small club called Nell's in Notting Hill and I was completely overwhelmed. I had no idea he was such a mesmerising performer and played great saxophone and keyboards. I haven't been impressed with an artist like this for many years. I'm always surprised at his ability to quote philosophers and thinkers like Aristotle, Kant, Socrates and Nietzsche.

Van leads a very disciplined life these days. He doesn't drink or take any drugs and insists that he won't go on stage later than 8pm. When he goes to America he makes sure he arrives a day or so before he needs to be there so he can get rid of his jet lag.

Last year I went with him to see Quincy Jones at the O2. When the interval came he said he couldn't believe how big the venue was. I said, 'I saw you here a little while ago, you can't be that surprised.' He explained to me that he goes from his dressing room to the stage and when he's finished he goes back to the dressing room and home. 'When the lights are in your eyes you could be anywhere.'

He doesn't suffer fools gladly and that's where his grumpy reputation kicks in. He expects his musicians to be as hard-working and as conscientious as he is. When it comes to interviews he expects the interviewer to be smart and not come up with the same old questions. When he goes into a restaurant he expects to eat and not wait till the waiter is in the mood to find his table.

We have written a bunch of songs together and it has been a joy to work with him because I know if he likes my idea he'll go with it and if he doesn't he won't. I usually give him a lyric and sometimes I'll ask him if he liked it and he'll casually say, 'I've recorded it.' This is the first song we wrote together:

VAN MORRISON

'Every Time I See a River'

Haven't heard your voice
In quite a while
Haven't seen you dance
Or seen you smile
I can go days when nothing is wrong
But it just doesn't last very long

Every time I see a river
Every time I hear a train
Every time I hear a sad song
It reminds me of what we had then
Every time I see a river
Feel like I'm back in love again

My life seems together
And I'm doing just fine
But I remember when I was yours
And you were mine
I don't need your picture on the wall
I don't need anything at all

Every time I see a river
Every time I hear a train
Every time I hear a sad song
It reminds me of what we had then
Every time I see a river
Feels like I'm back in love again
I just can't stand the pain

THE SANEST GUY IN THE ROOM

Haven't heard your voice
In quite a while
Haven't seen you dance
Or seen you smile
I can go days when nothing is wrong
But it just doesn't last very long

Every time I see a river
Every time I hear a train
Every time I hear a sad song
It reminds me of what we had then
Every time I see a river
Feel like I'm back in love again

THE DEATH OF GREAT SONGS

I would not join a march or wave placards for many causes. One would certainly be that every neighbourhood in England should have a Jewish deli. Another one I would demonstrate outside Downing Street for would be the preservation of the Great American Songbook. I am upset and worried about its rapid decline.

I'm reminded of something Billy Wilder said when he was editing his film *Buddy Buddy*. Christopher Hampton asked him how it was going and Billy said, 'The patient is on the operating table. We don't hold out much hope!'

Writer Michael Henderson put it well when he said, 'I fear that the next generation will never get to hear the best songs written in the twentieth century by the likes of Irving Berlin, Cole Porter, Rodgers and Hart and the rest. It is commendable for schoolchildren to learn about Mozart and Bach if they are to enjoy the emotional richness that great music can bring to life. But it would be no bad thing also to introduce them to the classic American songs. Something has to be done to avoid the collapse of this treasured art form.'

When I air my feelings people usually say, 'Yes, but time moves on.' I can't buy that argument. I have always made sure my grandchildren and my nephews are familiar with those songs.

My young nephew Roman is a pop singer who is a fan of singers I've never heard of and when he plays me their latest outpourings I then insist that he sits down and listens carefully to songs like Hoagy Carmichael's 'The Nearness of You', Jerome Kern's 'The Way You Look Tonight', the Gershwins' 'Someone to Watch Over Me', Rodgers and Hart's 'Where or When' or Cole Porter's 'Every Time We Say Goodbye'. It has taken me a few years to drum this into him but it has paid off. He now appreciates the skill and craftmanship that went into these copper-bottom standards.

The problem is that this generation never gets to hear or learn about them. The leading practitioners who introduced us to this treasure trove have all gone. Everything I ever learned about great songs came from the likes of Frank Sinatra, Vic Damone, Ella Fitzgerald, Billie Holiday, Sarah Vaughan and other gifted interpreters. These days there are only a few people still banging the drum for brilliantly constructed songs. Only two come instantly to mind, Tony Bennett, now in his nineties, and Jack Jones, also no spring chicken.

Michael Feinstein has created his own foundation, based in Carmel, Indiana, the sole purpose of which is to inspire and educate by celebrating the timeless standards of pop, jazz, Broadway and Hollywood. The organisation is dedicated to the preservation and promotion of the music of the Great American Songbook. So many of the songs written in this period had lyrics that were witty, sophisticated, tender or sad. I long to hear much more of these great songs from that period on the radio. If and when that happens I will do as Irving Berlin suggested – 'Face the Music and Dance'.

A little while ago I was at a music-industry dinner and I was chatting to Tim Rice, Van Morrison and Ray Davies of the Kinks. I'm pleased to say they all listen to my radio programme so I asked them if they had a favourite song from the Great American Songbook. I was really shocked because they all chose the same one – 'Smoke Gets in Your Eyes'.

MORE MUSICALS IN NO PARTICULAR ORDER

I say no particular order because when you look back on so many shows the timeline gets all hazy. I won't go into a forensic study of them all but as I probably spent years on them, I feel they're worth a mention. Incidentally, my devoted and supportive family saw them all and they felt about my work exactly as they felt about me when I was a stand-up comic – fabulous.

Song and Dance

It was Cameron Mackintosh's idea to combine Andrew's *Tell Me on a Sunday* album with his instrumental album *Variations*. The first half would be sung by Marti Webb and the second half would feature Wayne Sleep and a group of the best dancers in the country. It worked very well and ran for more than two years at the Palace Theatre in London. A revised version went to Broadway starring Bernadette Peters, and although Bernadette won a Tony award for her performance and Andrew and myself received a Tony nomination for the score, the show wasn't a patch on the London production. As I've said, *Tell Me on a Sunday* is about an ordinary girl from Muswell Hill who goes to New York to try and sort her life out. It's her ordinariness amid the madness of New York and Hollywood that is the reason the show touches a lot of nerves. The Broadway production was too polished and had slick orchestrations – a lot of the humanity of the piece was lost.

I put words to one of the *Variation* melodies and it was used in the second half. I called it 'Unexpected Song'.

> I have never felt like this
> For once I'm lost for words
> Your smile has really thrown me
> This is not like me at all
>
> I never thought I'd know
> The kind of love you've shown me
> Now, no matter where I am
> No matter what I do
> I see your face appearing
> Like an unexpected song
> An unexpecting song
> That only we are hearing
>
> I don't know what's going on
> Can't work it out at all
> Whatever made you choose me?
> I just can't believe my eyes
> You look at me as though
> You couldn't bear to lose me
>
> Now, no matter where I am
> No matter what I do
> I see your face appearing

Like an unexpected song
An unexpecting song
That only we are hearing

I have never felt like this
For once I'm lost for words
Your smile has really thrown me
This is not like me at all

I never thought I'd know
The kind of love you've shown me
Now, no matter where I am
No matter what I do
I see your face appearing
Like an unexpected song
An unexpected song
That only we are hearing

We have written *Tell Me* so many times that we decided a couple of years ago that there are so many different versions of it we should finally come up with a definitive one. Our final crack at it features 'Unexpected Song' as the encore number. We replaced it in the body of the show with a song called 'The Last Man in My Life'. We have both always been fond of this song and it seems to have a greater impact.

I'm a lady when you kiss me
I'm a child when you are leaving
I'm a woman every time our bodies meet

Complete

Long lost feelings stir inside me

Used to think nights were for sleeping

Being wanted is a thrill I never knew

Till you

Now I'm alive inside I'm glowing

I'm how I want to be

Loving you I can be me

Just me

It's the first time when you touch me

Now I long for rainy mornings

I am certain you're the last man in my life

Now I'm alive inside I'm glowing

I'm how I want to be

Loving you I can be me

Just me

It's the first time when you touch me

Now I long for rainy mornings

In each other we find all we're looking for

And more

Found the rainbow I was after

No more dreams with one face missing

I am certain you're the last man in my life

I am certain you're the last man in my life

Bonnie and Clyde

This was my second collaboration with the composer Frank Wildhorn. Frank has become known as the Andrew Lloyd

Webber of Asia. He has so many musicals playing in Korea and Japan. There was a time when he had three shows on Broadway in the same season. He's also very funny. He works out at the gym constantly and can lift 300 pounds without puffing. Leslie Bricusse calls him 'Frank the Tank'. Frank once said to me, 'I may not be as successful as Andrew or Stephen Schwartz or Alan Menken but I could kick the shit out of all of them!'

The show starred Jeremy Jordan and Laura Osnes as Bonnie and Clyde. They were both amazing and Laura picked up a Tony nomination for her performance. We also picked up a nomination for the score. It was a great success in La Jolla and Sarasota before arriving on Broadway in 2011. Frank describes the score as, 'non-traditional, a mixture of rockabilly, rhythm and blues and gospel music'. It didn't last long on Broadway which upset us all as it was building nicely and was becoming a sort of cult musical. It has since had many international productions and is scheduled to appear in London shortly. There is a song in the second act that always has people reaching for their tissues, especially elderly couples. It comes when Bonnie's sister-in-law, Blanche, tells Bonnie, 'You know when the police catch Clyde they're going to kill him and they'll kill you as well.' Bonnie says, 'I hope so,' and sings 'Dyin' Ain't So Bad'.

> Dyin' ain't so bad
> Not if you both go together
> Only when one's left alone does it get sad
> But a short and lovin' life
> That ain't so bad

MORE MUSICALS IN NO PARTICULAR ORDER

I only hope to God that I go first
I couldn't live on memories
I'm sorry, but I'm not that strong
There are some things in life
You can't replace
A love like ours don't happen twice
When all his days are through
Mine will be too

'Cos dyin' ain't so bad
Not if you both go together
Only when one's left behind does it get sad
But a short and lovin' life
That ain't so bad

I've met boys who talk about farms and horses
But they don't do much for me
I don't need to end up in a rockin' chair
Seems you get to live your life just once
And if that's how it's gonna be
Then I'd rather breathe in life than dusty air

Dyin' ain't so bad
Not if you both go together
Only when one's left alone does it get sad
But a short and lovin' life
A short and lovin' life
That ain't so bad.

There was another song in Bonnie and Clyde that was replaced in La Jolla. Strangely it was the second song in my career I have written about sexual dysfunction. The first one was 'Something Must Have Happened' from 'Maybe That's Your Problem'. This song was a duet with Bonnie and Clyde when they attempted to make love for the first time. Embarrassingly Clyde couldn't rise to the occasion. They sing 'This Never Happened Before'.

CLYDE

Feel sort of clumsy
I guess I'm rusty
Ain't done this since God knows when
It may take some little time babe
Till I raise hell again

BONNIE

Just hold me darlin'
That's all I'm needin'
You ain't got nothin' to prove
Just lyin' with you is fine babe
We'll spoil it if we move

CLYDE

I ain't been sleeping too good
But I'll soon be old lover boy Clyde

BONNIE

Don't worry, let's take it slow

One night at a time

Just stayin' close will keep me satisfied

Feel I'm in heaven

CLYDE

Feel that way too babe

This night should have been so much more

BONNIE

I told you, being with you is enough babe

BONNIE AND CLYDE

This never happened before

This never happened before.

Stephen Ward

This musical wasn't a commercial success and some people think the title is to blame. I believe it was the theatre – if it had opened at the more intimate Donmar or the Almeida I think it would have had a different outcome. People have come to expect that an Andrew Lloyd Webber musical will be a big glittering production. The musical is based on the 1963 Profumo affair, a British political scandal that originated with a sexual relationship in 1961, between John Profumo, the Secretary of State for War in Harold Macmillan's Conservative government, and Christine Keeler, a nineteen-year-old would-be model.

Once again I collaborated with Christopher Hampton, and once again we had a lot of fun writing this politically based show. It was also a joy to work with the brilliant director Richard Eyre. Most of the songs were very much what we call book songs, which means there's very little space to write a heartfelt ballad. However, there was one that we three and the critics thought was one of Andrew's best melodies. Unfortunately it is sung by Profumo's wife late in the show and we didn't know enough about her for the song to really land. We keep talking about revisiting the show and making some structural adjustments. The song comes when Mrs Profumo learns about her husband's infidelity and, this being a musical, she sings 'I'm Hopeless When It Comes To You'.

> My life is far from over
> Time to think about me
> I could live my life without you
> But what kind of a life would that be
> Part of me is saying I should go
> Maybe that's what I should do
> But I will not be leaving
> I'm hopeless when it comes to you
>
> You can't stay with him
> That's what they say
> And some days their words ring true
> But those are fleeting feelings
> I'm hopeless when it comes to you

You're bruised but you're not broken
There'll be no more lies
We'll go on together
Dry each other's eyes
This will make us stronger than before
Sometimes that's what pain can do
How could I think of leaving
I'm hopeless when it comes to you
How could I think of leaving
I'm hopeless when it comes to you

We're bruised but we're not broken
There'll be no more lies
We'll grow strong together
Dry each other's eyes

This will make us closer than before
Sometimes that's what pain can do
How could I think of leaving
I'm hopeless when it comes to you
I'm hopeless when it comes to you.

Dear Anyone

When we opened this show in Birmingham the critic there said it was the best British musical since *Oliver!* Something must have happened on the brief journey to the Cambridge Theatre in London . . . The story was about an agony aunt who could solve everyone's problems but her own. The book was by the wonderful Jack Rosenthal who I worked with on *Bar Mitzvah Boy*. The music was by Geoff Stephens, a hugely successful pop composer. We had a great cast; Jane Lapotaire was the agony aunt, Mercedes, and Stubby Kaye played a big part as her assistant. We thought we'd set the show in New York as it seemed to be the epicentre of the world when it comes to problem pages.

Once again we thought we had something special and the audiences loved it. We were very disappointed when it closed and have been trying to revive it for many years. We've come close and we don't intend to give up. One of the songs became a top ten hit for the group Hot Chocolate. It was produced by the legendary record producer Mickie Most. It was sung by our leading lady, the problem solver, and the cast who were the troubled letter writers. It's called 'I'll Put You Together Again'.

AGONY AUNT

When you can't take any more
When you think your life is over
Put down your tablets and pick up your pen
And I'll put you together again

If your faith withers away
If God can't bring you your answer
Write me a letter, I'll read it and then
I'll put you together again

CORRESPONDENTS

She'll put us together
Together again

MORE MUSICALS IN NO PARTICULAR ORDER

She'll put us together again
When things look hopeless
We tell her and then

AGONY AUNT

I'll put you together again

UPSET, NEW JERSEY

I've got a son who is queer

WORRIED, BROOKLYN

How do I stop Dad from drinking?

DESPERATE, LONG ISLAND

I think my kids know I entertain men

AGONY AUNT

I'll put you together again

REPENTANT

I raped a chick in Detroit

JOHN X

No one believes I shot Bobby

SADIE

I'll have a breakdown and what happens then?

THE SANEST GUY IN THE ROOM

AGONY AUNT

I'll put you together again

CORRESPONDENTS

She'll put us together again
She'll put us together again

AGONY AUNT

Drop me a few lines
I'll read them and then
I'll put you together again
No need to jump off a roof
I'll give you hope for the future
Scribble your hearts out
You'll soon say Amen
I'll put you together again

If there's no light anywhere
And you've got no one to turn to
I'll lead you out of the darkness and then
I'll put you together again

GIRL

Can a black woman have twins?

MAN

I'd love to come back as Joan Crawford

MAN

Can you get herpes by kissing a hen?

AGONY AUNT

I'll put you together again

BOY

How do I stop sniffing glue?

GIRL

Does he love me or my body?
I know why my boyfriend is called Big Ben

AGONY AUNT

I'll put you together again.

Dracula

Once again I collaborated with Christopher Hampton, with music by Frank Wildhorn. We opened at the La Jolla Playhouse in California. It played to 115 per cent capacity, the highest in that theatre's history. It didn't run as long as we hoped for on Broadway but since then has become a massive hit in Asia and other territories. This was one of Shirley's favourite scores and maybe the only one she wanted to hear time and time again.

The leading lady is called Mina and she is living a happy life with Jonathan Harker. When she meets Dracula, she is totally besotted and her well-ordered life is turned upside down.

My favourite song from the show comes when Mina is at her
most confused and sings to Dracula 'Please Don't Make Me
Love You'.

There's only so much

That a heart can take

Before it starts to break . . .

Please don't make me love you

Please don't make me need you

I've no room in my life

For something like this

Please don't take my mornings

Please don't steal my summers

I know they will vanish

The moment we kiss

I grow weak when we talk

I'm confused when we touch

I should just walk away

But that's asking too much

Please don't make me do this

Please don't make me want this

All my dreams were taken

Until I met you

You're the one I think of

Soon as I awaken

Funny how the heart

Tells the mind what to do

I'm not sure I could go through

All the joy and the pain
Much better not to let my dreams take flight

Please don't make me love you
Please don't make me need you
Simplify my life
Just by setting me free
Promise me you'll do this
Only you can do this
Please don't make me love you
Unless you love me.

Brighton Rock

I'd love to have another crack at this. It's a fantastic story about a psychopathic teenage hoodlum called Pinkie Brown. John Barry wrote the music, Giles Havergal wrote the book. And it was directed by Michael Attenborough. On reflection I think this story about murder and Catholic sin should have been done as an opera, much in the style of Sweeney Todd. It worked best when Pinkie soliloquised about his feelings around his rotten childhood and his hatred of life as in this song called 'Some Things Never Leave You'.

Some things never leave you
They stick in your brain
Round and round they go
Like a music hall refrain
'Mum and Dad are fighting,
Quick! Behind the chairs

THE SANEST GUY IN THE ROOM

Teacher's gonna hit me
For refusing to say prayers'

Some things never leave you
They're with you for good
Dad is getting legless
Down at the Robin Hood
Mum is smoking Players
Like some painted whore
'Keep your bleedin' voice down
There are coppers at the door'

I can hear Mum crying
Dad is talking tough
Don't care where I run to
I have heard enough

Saturday's like clockwork
In the other bed
The panting and the grinding
Is still inside my head
Is it pain or pleasure
What is going on?
I don't understand it
But I'm grateful when it's gone

Power is the one thing
People understand
You get more respect

With a razor in your hand
I've been carving squealers
Since I was so high
Some things never leave you
Somethings never leave you
Some things never leave you
Till you die.

Mrs Henderson Presents

This was one of my favourite projects and the audiences seemed to lap it up. It had five-star reviews but only ran for about five months at the Cambridge Theatre in London. The music was by George Fenton and Simon Chamberlain. The lesson learned from this show is that it's very hard to keep a show going if it doesn't have a big star name in it. I'm pleased to say that plans are afoot to bring it back. The story is about the Windmill Theatre which became a huge success when Mrs Henderson had her epiphany moment by deciding the Windmill girls should appear nude! Of course she had to convince the strict censorship of the Lord Chamberlain. This was done in a song sung by her and the censor Thomas Cromer. It was a very funny sequence and went something like this:

CROMER

I'll not endorse this moral degradation
There are things the world should never see
Plays about adultery and women's liberation
A three-act play about the last apostle

THE SANEST GUY IN THE ROOM

And the plot twist that I almost missed
Jesus as a communist!
The effrontery's colossal
Inflammatory drivel,
Offensive to the core
I can't get past the title
'Tis Pity She's A Whore
God Ibsen is so dark
So melancholy
Those Swedish writers are a gloomy lot
This one's got a vile plot
Anything but jolly

SECRETARY

In fact Sir, Mr Ibsen comes from Norway

CROMER

Everybody makes the same mistake
What earthly difference does that make?
I care not, have it your way
Scandinavia is to blame
Those endless nights
Woe betide the writer
Who can't see what he writes

I'm the guardian of the establishment
And the morals of the nation
I stand for common decency

The keeper of the flame

With my guiding hand

Art will not descend

Into squalid depravation

I'll protect England's good name

There are many things on which I will not waver

Prince Hamlet in a leather thong

A Doll's House set in old Hong Kong

With a masochistic flavour

A censor must protect the working classes

(Picking up a book)

Look! A left-wing *Charlie's Aunt*

With a homosexual slant

MRS HENDERSON

Oh I wish I had my glasses

CROMER

There's much I will allow

I am no prude

But never lissom ladies

Cavorting in the nude

MRS HENDERSON

But a censor should encourage innovation

CROMER

I live in fear of opening nights

263

I've never been forgiven
For that Jewish *Wuthering Heights*!
You're asking too much
It isn't fair
Bums and boobs all dancing
To the 'Londonderry Air'

MRS HENDERSON

Oh Tommy dear
We're of a single mind
We're talking grace and beauty
Not of bump and grind

CROMER

But is it art?

MRS HENDERSON

Well it's not music hall
There's nothing rude about a nude
That's in a painting on the wall

CROMER

I've not heard that before
It's worth debating
No hint of any motion
Every inch completely static
Not a single thing pulsating

MRS HENDERSON

The Windmill stage will be like a museum
Think of Rubens and Renoir up there

CROMER

Those two are my favourite pair

MRS HENDERSON

Please do try the camembert

CROMER

It's such a big decision
I can't be rushed
So don't be disappointed
If all your hopes are crushed

MRS HENDERSON

Now Tommy dear
This will be so much fun
I guarantee our little show
Won't worry anyone

CROMER

I have your word?

w HENDERSON

I'll say it once again
They will not move, they will not move

They'll have to breathe

But only now and then

CROMER

Then providing nothing's moving

I will approve

But I'll close you down at once

If any titties move

SECRETARY

He'll close you down at once

If any titties move!

While it's hard to keep a show going if it doesn't have a big name in it, and it is often said that a big star in a musical will guarantee a success, that's not always necessarily so. Katharine Hepburn playing Coco Chanel with a score by Alan Jay Lerner and André Previn opened on Broadway in 1969 and ran for 329 performances, which wasn't anything like the investors were hoping for. The great Richard Rodgers and the megastar Danny Kaye seemed an indestructible combination. They got together for the musical *Two By Two* which opened on Broadway in 1970 and ran for only ten months. It proves that if the story and the score don't work all the wishful thinking and irrational faith will only lead to heartache. *Two By Two* was based on Clifford Odets' retelling of the legend of Noah's Ark. The show didn't stay afloat for very long.

Budgie

Before I talk about the musical I want to talk about my amazing musical collaborator Mort Shuman. Mort was a big man. So big, in fact, his towering body housed many musical talents. There was the Nashville Mort, in a ten-gallon hat, snakeskin boots, picking out tunes on a coffee-stained guitar. There was the Parisienne Mort singing songs in French to sophisticated nightclub audiences. There was the Harlem Mort who loved to hang out with black musicians, smokin' and drinkin' till he dropped. There were many more Morts, all of them with an unquenchable lust for life.

He wrote twenty-four songs for Elvis Presley, but he also wrote for Janis Joplin, Ray Charles and Fats Domino. He had too many hits to mention but here's a few to give you an idea of his range: 'Save the Last Dance for Me', 'Viva Las Vegas', 'Can't Get Used to Losing You' and 'Teenager In Love'.

Budgie didn't get us the Tony Award we were hoping for but we had a wonderful time together. It was based on the television series starring Adam Faith. I have mixed emotions about Adam. In rehearsals he was always on the phone doing some business deal. He had a regular table at Fortnum and Mason where he used to hang out with hedge fund managers and stockbrokers. He was very good in the show but wouldn't do anything to publicise it. He used to say, 'Before I do anything I ask myself would Marlon Brando do it?' This was very frustrating but I called him one day and said to him Marlon Brando is on the Gloria Hunniford show on Saturday!

The show was set in and around a seedy Soho club and the characters were mainly gangsters and strippers. Budgie's love interest was Hazel, played beautifully by Anita Dobson. Mort's favourite song from the show was a sad ballad that Hazel sings about her relationship with a lowlife like Budgie. It's called 'In One of My Weaker Moments':

All the good times that we had
I could count on one hand
People say that I'm crazy
People don't understand
I keep saying I'll leave him
I almost do but then
Every time I head for the door
I think it through again . . .

In one of my weaker moments
I let the moment go
I'll never change him
Why I stay here I don't know

In one of my weaker moments
I let the moment die
Seems when you love someone
You can't say goodbye

It's not how I imagined
Waiting up half the night
How long can you keep hoping
We're gonna get it right?
When I think of the future

I want to fly away
Now's the time, yes, I could go now
That's what I always say
In one of my weaker moments
I let the moment go
I'll never change him
Why I stay here I don't know

In one of my weaker moments
I let the moment die
Seems when you love someone
You can't say goodbye

In one of my weaker moments
I say there's nothing wrong
I hide the feelings
I've been feeling for too long
In one of my weaker moments
I say let's wait and see
For I know if I go
He won't come running after me

The Little Prince and the Aviator

John Barry and I had high hopes for this show. It was based on the classic book by Antoine de Saint-Exupery. The book for the musical was written by Hugh Wheeler who also wrote the books for *Sweeney Todd* and *A Little Night Music*. It starred Michael York, who was a major movie star. The show opened at the Alvin Theatre in New York in January 1982.

During a long preview period we rewrote many songs and the script kept changing but we felt that audiences were enjoying it. One unforgettable day I was in my room at the Mayflower Hotel and I switched on the television news and heard the presenter, Sue Simmons, announce that *The Little Prince and the Aviator* had been cancelled. We had gone through all the gruelling rehearsals and previews and were totally stunned. John and his wife Laurie and Shirley and me all met to talk about this and sort of drown our sorrows.

It turned out that the producer Joe Tandet was forced to close the show by the Nederlander organisation who demanded more money than they originally asked for to keep the show open through the final week of previews – Joe Tandet sued them and won. He was awarded a million dollars.

ABBAcadabra/Whistle Down the Wind/Romeo and Juliet/The Goodbye Girl/Dance of the Vampires/Starlight Express

I've lumped all these shows together because I only had a small involvement with most of them.

ABBAcadabra started out as a children's television show in France based on the songs of ABBA. It was put together by Alain Boublil. Cameron Mackintosh produced it and it played at the Lyric Theatre in London for a sell-out eight-week season. I did various lyrics to the great Abba melodies. It starred Elaine Paige who worked with me again in spite of *Maybe That's Your Problem*. There is often talk of a revival.

Whistle Down the Wind was written by Andrew and Jim Steinman. When producer Bill Kenwright took the show on tour he asked me to write a couple of songs based on the Bible for it.

Romeo and Juliet was something I wish I had never got involved with. The French producers flew me to Belgium to see it in some vast arena where it was a monumental success. Thousands of people were singing all the words and every song got a standing ovation. The show had this reaction in many countries. I couldn't help being overwhelmed by the response. However, I learned that you shouldn't tamper with Shakespeare in this way in England. Jane McDonald was terrific as the nurse.

The Goodbye Girl played on Broadway and I was asked to add lyrics for the English run. The book was by Neil Simon and the music by Marvin Hamlisch. It starred Gary Wilmott. I did enjoy writing this piece and it was well worth doing just to meet Neil Simon and the unstoppable Marvin.

Dance of the Vampires was Jim Steinman's major epic work that played Broadway starring Michael Crawford. I only wrote one big power ballad with Jim called 'Braver Than We Are'.

I had an urgent call one day from Andrew Lloyd Webber because he wanted to add a new duet to *Starlight Express*. He was anxious to get this in the show and I remember writing it overnight. It was called 'Next Time You Fall In Love':

> I guess I'm not too good
> At keeping love alive for long
> I think I've found the answers
> But the answer's always wrong
> My first love was my true love
> And it should have been my last
> The only time I'm happy's
> When I'm dreaming in the past

THE SANEST GUY IN THE ROOM

Next time you fall in love
It better be with me
The way it used to be
Back then was when
We touched the starlight

Sometimes you turn away
From what your heart tells you is right
And so you settle for
Whatever gets you through the night
The flame you thought was dead
May suddenly begin to burn
And broken hearts can be repaired
That's something that you learn

Next time you fall in love
It better be with me
The way it used to be
Back then was when
We touched the starlight

I've relived every moment
That I ever shared with you
What fools we were to end a dream
That looked like coming true

Next time you fall in love
It better be with me
The way it used to be

Back then was when

We touched the starlight

I guess I'm not too good

At keeping love alive for long

I think I've found the answers

But the answer's always wrong

My first love was my true love

And it should have been my last

The only time I'm happy's

When I'm dreaming in the past

Next time you fall in love

It better be with me

The way it used to be

Back then was when

We touched the starlight

Feather Boy

Debbie Wiseman and myself started on this thirteen years ago! It is finally coming to fruition and the producers promise us it will be produced very shortly. It started life as a children's novel by Nicky Singer. The book won Blue Peter's Book of the Year in 2002. It was commissioned by the National Theatre for Shell Connections, its nationwide festival of youth theatre. It played in about twenty-five youth theatre groups up and down the land before it played at the National itself. I've always been fond of this story. In a nutshell it's about a group of children who go to visit an old people's home. They learn things from each other.

Mavis is suffering from the onset of dementia and sings 'It's Still Me In Here'.

THE SANEST GUY IN THE ROOM

My eyes are not as bright, my skin is not as tight,
But it's still me in here

My knees hurt me a lot, my mem'ry's gone to pot,
But it's still me in here

On the outside I may look a little worse for wear,
Forget my face ignore my hands, you shouldn't be looking there

I may be old and lame but part of me's stayed the same,
How do I make it clear that it's still me in here?

I've learned that you can't judge a book by its cover,
You have to read the pages.
I've also learned that a loving heart never ages

Though I am not as strong and the future's not as long
Some things don't disappear, yes it's still me in here,
Yes it's still me in here.

I can't eat fancy meals
And I've stopped wearing heels
But it's still me in here

My blood is very thin
I get lipstick on my chin
But it's still me in here

Growing old is not so bad it isn't what it seems
You'll be surprised to learn that age
Has nothing to do with dreams

Though I am not as strong
And the future's not as long
Some things don't disappear
Yes it's still me in here

Also in the care home is a charming elderly man who has feelings for Dulcie. He tries to express them in 'A Handful of Aprils':

There is one thing old people don't mention
So it remains unsaid
We spend too much time looking back
And waste the few years that lie ahead . . .
A handful of Aprils
A teaspoon of tomorrows
A small box of dreams
Let me share them with you
We still have time to make one or two come true

Only the moon and stars keep on shining
Time doesn't matter
They stay as they are
They are on a never-ending journey
But our journey only takes us so far . . .

A handful of Aprils
A teaspoon of tomorrows
A small box of dreams
Let me share them with you
We still have time to make one or two come true.

The Third Man

George Fenton, Christopher Hampton and myself have been on this for a few years now. It's had a couple of workshops in Vienna. Trevor Nunn has joined us and we are hopeful of a production in our lifetimes! It's based on one of the best British films ever made, which starred Orson Welles as Harry Lime and was written by Graham Greene. The film was famous for its musical theme played on the zither, known all over the world as 'The Harry Lime Theme'. In the film, the character Anna is an actress but as it is a musical we decided to make her a cabaret singer. This is her first somewhat saucy song that she sings at The Casanova Club, a dingy basement with a dubious-looking overdressed clientele – mostly black marketeers with their molls.

'A Second Opinion'

I was madly in love with Klaus

I longed to become his spouse

But Klaus kept telling me

My skirts were too short

My sweaters were too tight

My heels were much too high

My lipstick way too bright

So I went out with Paul

Who didn't agree with Klaus at all

Paul liked my neckline low

He likes me drinking beer

Paul likes me in a skirt

That goes right up to here

MORE MUSICALS IN NO PARTICULAR ORDER

Klaus was always so prim
I tried to explain to him
Although I went with Paul
I did not love him at all . . .

It was only for a second opinion
A second opinion that's all
So should I change my ways for Klaus
Or be myself with Paul?

In bed Klaus is a gent
In fact he's too polite
His movements never change
I wondered if that was right
But Paul likes to play games
He's daring and he's bad
He's found some parts of me
I never knew I had

It was only for a second opinion
A second opinion that's all
Why should I change my ways with Klaus
When I feel so great with Paul

My advice to all you ladies
Whose lives are as boring as hell
Is always get a second opinion
Maybe a third one as well!

MY TOP TEN MUSICALS

West Side Story is about as good as it gets. The story is based on *Romeo and Juliet* and was written by Arthur Laurents, the score was by Leonard Bernstein and Stephen Sondheim, and it was directed and choreographed by Jerome Robbins. It took about ten years to reach the stage. There are loads of books about how it was put together so I'll not get into all that. What I find interesting is that Leonard Bernstein wanted to write the lyrics himself but he was too busy. He offered the job to Betty Comden and Adolphe Green who turned it down. Arthur Laurents heard the score to a show called *Saturday Night* with words and music by Sondheim. He didn't like the music but liked the lyrics. Sondheim's initial reaction when he was offered the job wasn't happy because he wanted to write his own words and music. It was Oscar Hammerstein who persuaded him to take it on as it would be great experience working with Leonard, Arthur and Jerry.

Sondheim didn't get on great with Arthur Laurents. Many years later at some award ceremony, Arthur was introduced as 'a living legend'. Sondheim was heard to say, 'Wrong on both counts.'

Why do I like it so much? It has everything, great romance, danger and tragedy and there isn't a word or note that isn't integral to the story. Sometimes when you hear a song many times you sort of take it for granted, but I urge you to listen to the song 'Tonight' with fresh ears because love songs as passionate as this one don't come along too often.

MARIA AND TONY

Tonight, tonight
The world is wild and bright
Going mad
Shooting stars into space
Today the world was just an address
A place for me to live in
No better than all right

But here you are
And what was just a world
Is a star
Tonight

The musical *Guys and Dolls* is based on two short stories by Damon Runyon. The score was written by Frank Loesser, the book by Abe Burrows and it was directed by George Kaufman. It opened on Broadway in 1950 and won the Best Musical Award for that season. The story concerns gamblers, gangsters and other members of the New York underworld. The characters had colourful names such as Nathan Detroit, Nicely Nicely Johnson and Sky Masterson. The show has its own Runyonesque language and the songs have wit and heart. This is no surprise to me as Frank Loesser has been one of my favourite lyric writers ever since I began noticing him. He wrote the songs 'Baby It's Cold

Outside', 'Two Sleepy People', 'Slow Boat to China', 'I Don't Want to Walk Without You', 'Spring Will Be a Little Late This Year' and dozens more. He also wrote the musicals *Where's Charley?*, *How to Succeed In Business Without Really Trying*, *Hans Christian Andersen* and *The Most Happy Fella*.

He was supposed to have been a pretty difficult man to work with. He once hit a soprano in the mouth for not singing one of his songs properly. He later apologised by giving the lady a diamond bracelet. During the rehearsals of *Guys and Dolls* he told the director that he wanted his songs reprised in the second half. The director replied, 'I'll reprise your songs if you let me reprise the jokes.' The score has many show-stopping songs – 'Sit Down You're Rocking the Boat', 'Adelaide's Lament', 'I've Never Been In Love Before' and 'Bushel and a Peck'. I've always loved the imagery and desperation in the song 'Luck Be a Lady'. It comes in the second act and is sung by Sky Masterson. He has fallen in love with the beautiful and pious Sarah Brown who runs The Save The Soul Mission. Her mission is to get all sinners to repent. Sky, who will bet on anything, bets his gambling friends that he will pay them all $1000 if he loses but if he wins all of them must attend a revival meeting at the mission. He has a lot at stake, blows on the dice and sings 'Luck Be a Lady'. Incidentally, this was sung by Marlon Brando in the film which upset Frank Sinatra because he thought it was the best song in the film. He then started to sing it in his act just to prove he could sing it better than Brando.

Luck be a lady tonight
Luck be a lady tonight

Luck if you've ever been a lady to begin with

Luck be a lady tonight

I was lucky enough to meet Frank Sinatra a couple of times. I was friendly with his record producer Jimmy Bowen, who was married to Keely Smith, and he invited me to one of Frank's recording sessions. It was quite a strange experience as there was an audience there. Frank liked to sing to people as opposed to an empty recording studio. At that session Yul Brynner was taking pictures of Frank throughout the session. It was all a bit surreal. For the life of me I've been trying to think of the song Frank sang but I can't because this was the time in Frank's career when he recorded some very bad poppy songs in the hope of trying to get a commercial hit. Thankfully that period went by and he went back to the Sinatra we know and love.

I remember Marvin Hamlisch saying to me that he wrote around sixty songs for *A Chorus Line* though only about fifteen were used. He said it was thrilling but utterly exhausting working with the director Michael Bennett. I met Michael a few times – we were often working in adjoining rehearsal rooms in New York. He was hugely admired as a brilliant dancer, choreographer and director. When I saw *A Chorus Line* I couldn't believe that no one ever thought of this idea before. It's about a group of talented dancers who are auditioning for a part in an upcoming musical. Each one of them talks about their life and we get to know all about their deepest fears and how and why they want to get this job. All seventeen of them have a story to tell, some amusing and some heartbreaking. The show was a huge success and won nine Tony Awards plus the Pulitzer prize for drama. What made this show unique was the fact that there were no stars in it and no set. It was played out on a bare stage. This is what a Broadway producer dreams of. It became the longest-running show in Broadway history. That record stood until *Cats* broke it many years later. The lyrics were written by Edward Kleban, who never wrote anything noteworthy before. He said, 'It took me a year to write the words and I only got five hundred dollars for a year's work.' He also said, 'I didn't know if that would be it or I'd make a fortune.' We all know the answer to that.

When the final eight dancers are selected, their ordinary day clothes are replaced by identical gold spangled costumes and they sing and dance to the show's big hit number.

> One singular sensation
> Every little step she takes
> One thrilling combination
> Every move that she makes
> One smile and suddenly
> Nobody else will do

It was a life-changing experience when I saw Zero Mostel in *Fiddler on the Roof* on Broadway in the late sixties. From that moment on I knew I wanted to have a go at writing musicals. I always wanted to meet Sheldon Harnick, the man who wrote those lyrics, for two reasons. He wrote great lyrics and he was once married to a favourite comedy actress of mine, Elaine May. I did get to meet him a few times and he was as warm and witty as his lyrics. He was also a great singer. I saw him in cabaret in New York and was surprised at how good he was. I can only think of Johnny Mercer as another lyric writer who sang well.

The music was by Jerry Bock, who often told the story of when the show went to Japan and was a huge success. A Japanese member of the audience went up to him and said, 'How do you think this will play in New York?'

The story is about Tevye, a poor Jewish milkman with five daughters. There are so many wonderful songs in the show including 'If I Were a Rich Man', 'Tradition', 'Matchmaker, Matchmaker', 'To Life' and 'Do You Love Me'. But I've chosen the song that is sung at one of the daughters' weddings. It is sung by Tevye and his wife Golde. I defy any caring parent not to be moved by this song.

> Sunrise, sunset
> Sunrise, sunset
> Quickly flow the days
> Seedlings turn overnight to sunflowers
> Blossoming even as we gaze

If I could have dinner with anyone living or dead, and Santa Claus wasn't available, I would choose Irving Berlin. It's hard to believe that he couldn't speak a word of English when he arrived in New York from Russia aged five. He is regarded as probably the best songwriter America has produced. I've chosen *Annie Get*

Your Gun as one of my favourite musicals mainly because of the number of great songs that are in it. The story is a fictionalised version of the life of sharpshooter Annie Oakley and her romance with fellow sharpshooter Frank Butler.

Irving Berlin almost pulled out of writing the score. He called up Oscar Hammerstein and said, 'I can't write all these hill billy lyrics.' Oscar said to him, 'All you have to do is leave off the g's.' That night Irving wrote 'Doin' What Comes Naturally'. Some other songs he wrote for the show are 'There's No Business Like Show Business', 'The Girl That I Marry', 'Anything You Can Do', 'They Say It's Wonderful' and 'You Can't Get a Man With a Gun'. My favourite song from the show also happens to be one of my favourite songs of all time. It comes early in the second act when Annie realises she has fallen in love and sings 'I Got Lost In His Arms'.

> I got lost in his arms
> And I had to stay
> It was dark in his arms
> And I lost my way

Oklahoma! was a game changer. It put an end to earlier musicals where all-purpose songs were used – songs that didn't necessarily follow the story's narrative but were shoehorned in. They were usually wonderful songs but could have fitted any show. In *Oklahoma!* every song served a dramatic purpose and became an essential part of the story. It was critically slammed when it opened out of town – the powerful and influential columnist Walter Winchell wrote 'No gags, no girls, no chance.'

Oklahoma! was the first joint adventure for Richard Rodgers and Oscar Hammerstein, and after twenty-three hectic years of working with the wayward Larry Hart, Richard really enjoyed the calmness that came with his new collaborator. With Larry Hart the music always came first but Oscar wrote the lyrics first and Richard Rodgers preferred this way of working. As we all know *Oklahoma!* was an enormous hit and after glowing reviews Richard and Oscar walked by the theatre and were thrilled to see lengthy queues at the box office. Richard said, 'Shall we go somewhere quiet where we can talk or should we go to Sardi's and show off?' Oscar thought about it and said, 'Hell, let's go to Sardi's and show off.'

I love the score, which includes so many memorable songs: 'Surrey with the Fringe on Top', 'Oklahoma' and 'Oh What a Beautiful Morning'. Oscar Hammerstein was asked about the line he wrote in 'Oh What a Beautiful Morning', the one that goes, 'The corn is as high as an elephant's eye.' The interviewer said did that line come to you on the spur of the moment? Oscar said, 'Nothing comes to me on the spur of the moment. What comes first are thousands of moments of thoughts.'

My favourite song from the show comes when Curly, a cowboy who is in love with Laurey, asks her to go to the box social dance with him. She has already said she'll go with Jud who is a lonely disturbed farm hand who has become obsessed with Laurey. Afraid to tell Jud she won't go with him, Laurey tries to convince Curly and herself that she does not love him. I always marvel at the way Oscar Hammerstein manages to say something fresh and interesting about love that hasn't been said before.

Don't throw bouquets at me

Don't please my folks too much

Don't laugh at my jokes too much

People will say we're in love

After the opening night of *Oklahoma!*, Alan Jay Lerner sent Oscar Hammerstein a telegram which read, 'I cried twice last night, once at your wonderful show and again when I realised it had nothing to do with me!' Andrew Lloyd Webber told me that when he was speaking to Her Majesty the Queen, she told him that she adored the song 'People Will Say We're In Love' from the show. I think that last sentence may have taken name-dropping to a whole new level.

Andrew Lloyd Webber and Cameron Mackintosh have proved to be great collaborators and also great competitors in the world of musical theatre. It's odd that both of them have the same favourite song. It's 'Some Enchanted Evening' from *South Pacific*. I've been in Andrew's company many times when he has extolled Richard Rodgers as the greatest melodist of all time. I was at a dinner with Cameron recently and I asked him what his favourite song is as I wanted to play it on my radio show. Before I could finish the sentence he said, 'Some Enchanted Evening'. As Oscar Hammerstein says in his brilliant lyric, 'Fools give you reasons, wise men never try.'

The score is full of wonderful songs that have become standards including 'There Is Nothing Like a Dame', 'I'm Gonna Wash That Man Right Outa My Hair', 'Younger Than Springtime', 'A Cockeyed Optimist' and 'I'm in Love with a Wonderful Guy'.

The plot revolves around Nellie, an American nurse stationed on a South Pacific island. She falls in love with Emile, a middle-aged expatriate French plantation owner, but struggles to accept his mixed-race children by his first wife, now deceased. Nellie is unable to overcome her deep-seated racial prejudices and tearfully leaves Emile. He is left to reflect sadly on what might have been. 'Some Enchanted Evening' is a powerful and touching end to Act One.

> Some enchanted evening
> When you find your true love
> When you feel her call you
> Across a crowded room
> Then fly to her side
> And make her your own
> Or all through your life
> You may dream all alone
> Once you have found her
> Never let her go
> Once you have found her
> Never let her go

Richard Rodgers once wrote that *Carousel* was the favourite of all his musicals. *Time* magazine named it as the best musical of the twentieth century. If you don't cry at the end when Billy Bigelow sings 'If I Loved You' then you haven't got a pulse.

There are so many emotional moments in this show that bring a tear to your eye. When Billy's wife Julie tells him she's pregnant and he realises that he will become a father he gets to sing his 'Soliloquy', one of the greatest songs ever written for a musical. Another tissue-reaching moment is when Billy dies in the second act and all the characters try to comfort Julie with the landmark anthem, 'You'll Never Walk Alone'.

On his way to heaven Billy meets the Starmaker, a heavenly official, who tells him that the good he did on earth was not enough to get him into heaven. The Starmaker says he will allow Billy into heaven if he can redeem himself and he allows Billy one day back on earth. His daughter Louise is now fifteen and has had a lifetime of people talking about her dead father as a wife-beater and murderer. Billy introduces himself as a friend of her father. He also gives a star that he stole from heaven to his sobbing daughter. She refuses it, and, frustrated, he slaps her hand. He then makes himself invisible. Louise tells her mother Julie what happened but she said that the slap felt more like a kiss. Julie understands her perfectly. Louise retreats to the house and Julie notices the star Billy dropped; she picks it up and feels Billy's presence. This is where Billy sings 'If I Loved You', a reprise of the song he sang to Julie when they met. This is also the moment, when I was watching the film with Christopher Hampton and Andrew at Andrew's villa in Cap Ferrat, that the three of us cried in unison.

If I loved you
Time and again
I would try to say
All I'd want you to know
If I loved you

Alan Jay Lerner went through lyrical hell while writing *My Fair Lady*. He did this quite often. André Previn worked with Alan on a musical called *Coco* starring Katharine Hepburn, and said, 'Alan takes longer to write a lyric than it takes for an elephant to have a baby.' He tried to come up with a lyric for 'Wouldn't It Be Loverly' but nothing popped into his head. He attempted this day after day with no results. After a month of biting nails and losing eight pounds, in desperation he went to see psychiatrist and respected analyst Bela Mittelman. In his book *The Street Where I Live*, he says, 'He was the only psychiatrist I ever met who had a sense of humour and did not have modern furniture in his waiting room.' Mr. Mittelman said to him, 'You write as if your life depends on every line.' Alan replied, 'It does.' During the hour-long consultation, he got Alan to talk about his recent past and Alan told him about an incident concerning the great star Mary Martin and her husband Richard Halliday. Apparently they read that Alan and his musical partner Frederick Loewe were writing *My Fair Lady* and Mary would be interested in playing the part of Eliza Doolittle. Alan and Fritz, as he was called, didn't think she was right for the part but as she was such a huge star they thought they should meet her and play her the five songs they had written. They did this and there was no reaction from Mary or Richard. After five days Alan couldn't stand the suspense any longer so he called Richard who suggested they have lunch at the Hampshire House.

Richard told Alan that Mary walked the floor half the night saying over and over again, 'How could this have happened? Richard, those dear boys have lost their talent.' Alan told Mr Mittelman that the words 'Those dear boys have lost their talent' were forever engraved on the walls of his duodenal lining. 'Mr Mittelman began to chuckle and in an instant I realised that that brutal lunch in the Hampshire House had shaken me more profoundly than I realised.' At 6.30 the next morning Alan completed the lyric.

The reviews for the show were uniformly ecstatic. Brooks Atkinson in the *New York Times* called it, 'A wonderful show.' The *Herald Tribune* proclaimed it, 'A miraculous musical.' I find the piece impossible to resist. The story of a professor and a flower girl falling in love to unforgettable music and lyrics gets me every time I see it. It's hard to choose a favourite out of 'On the Street Where You Live', 'With a Little Bit of Luck', 'I Could Have Danced All Night', etc. But I've gone for 'I've Grown Accustomed to Her Face'.

Alan once told me that he wrote pages and pages of dialogue for Professor Higgins to express his love for Eliza, but in the end he found no words were necessary. You just had to watch the professor looking angry, bewildered and thoughtful and with the melody of 'I Could Have Danced All Night' being played it would be enough to warm the coldest heart. Alan was a master of coming up with these everyday phrases that soared when they were sung.

I've grown accustomed to her face

She almost makes the day begin

I've grown accustomed to the tune

She whistles night and noon

Her smiles, her frowns

Her ups, her downs

Are second nature to me now

Cary Grant's real name was Archie Leach and he said that Cary Grant was a completely made-up character that he'd been playing all those years. A friend of his said to him one day 'I've always wanted to be Cary Grant.' And he said, 'So did I!' He was offered the Rex Harrison part in *My Fair Lady* and turned it down. Jack Warner, the producer, offered him a fortune but he said to Mr Warner, 'That part belongs to Rex Harrison and if you don't give it to him, I won't even go to see it.'

Irving Berlin and Cole Porter didn't make many mistakes when it came to choosing a subject for a musical. Strangely they both declined to write the score for *Gypsy*. The job eventually went to Jule Styne and Stephen Sondheim.

I remember having lunch with Jule one day at Trader Vic's in the Hilton Hotel in London, and I asked him if he enjoyed working with Sondheim. He said the man's a fucking genius but he doesn't give a shit about writing hit songs! He said, 'Take the song "Small World", there's a line in it where the girl in the show sings "I'm a woman with children". I told Steve that means no man can sing it.'

A few years later Steve changed the line to 'I'd love to have children', Johnny Mathis recorded it and it became the hit that Jule was hoping for.

There have been many shows about show business including *Funny Girl*, *42nd Street* and *Kiss Me Kate* but *Gypsy* is by far my favourite. It is loosely based on the memoirs of Gypsy Rose Lee, the famous striptease artist, and focuses on her mother, Rose, who is the ultimate stage mother; ambitious, controlling and deluded. I've met people like Rose over the years, and, although not as terrifying as the character in the show, some of them come pretty close.

The show was praised to the hilt when it opened on Broadway. Ben Brantley of the *New York Times* said, 'This may be the greatest of all American musicals.' It is laden with wonderful witty and poignant songs including 'Everything's Coming Up Roses', 'Small World', 'All I Need Is the Girl' and the magnificent 'Rose's Turn'. Stephen Sondheim's lyrics are dazzling, particularly in the song 'Together'. Any lyric writers out there should take a good hard look at them and marvel at his lyrical dexterity. It's sung by Rose and Herbie, who will be managing the girls, and Louise, Rose's daughter:

ROSE

Wherever we go, whatever we do
We're gonna go through it together
We may not go far, but sure as a star
Wherever we are it's together

Wherever I go, I know he goes

Wherever I go, I know she goes

No fits, no fights, no feuds

And no egos, amigos, together!

SUNSET BOULEVARD

This was a dream assignment for me. I remember seeing the film as a boy at the Regal Cinema in Hackney. I fell in love with a bunch of old film-noir films then; *The Third Man*, *Double Indemnity* and *The Big Sleep* come to mind. After *Tell Me on a Sunday* Andrew asked me to come to a screening of *Sunset Boulevard* in Dean Street as he was thinking of turning it into a musical. We wrote a couple of songs, one was called 'Madam Takes a Lot of Looking After', which was written for Max, the long-suffering first husband of Norma Desmond. The other song was for Norma to sing and it was called 'One Star'. Andrew later used the melody for his *Cats* musical and it was retitled 'Memory'.

Andrew wanted Christopher Hampton to write the book but Christopher wanted to write the lyrics as well. I then had lunch with Christopher and we decided we'd do the whole thing together. Christopher is always busy – I don't think he's ever had a fallow period in his life. In order to deal with the other projects he was involved with it was decided that the three of us would spend the first week of every month at Andrew's villa in Cap Ferrat. It was a very happy time and most of the work was written in six sessions. Once Andrew has an idea for a musical he gets very impatient to get going. I remember his frustration at Christopher's unavailability. In a way Christopher and myself are a bit like that so when we got together we didn't waste any time in getting stuck in.

What I loved the most about the story of *Sunset* was that everyone can relate to it. It has that universal theme that I always try to find in a song. Everyone can relate to a major star of yesteryear whose glory days are over. We see it all the time in show business but no one likes to admit that their best days are behind them. Norma, whose mind is adrift, believes her best days are ahead of her and this insanity is both heartbreaking and amusing to watch.

Norma's first song in the musical is when Joe Gillis, a struggling screenwriter, accidentally chooses her driveway to escape from some angry finance men who are trying to repossess his car. Norma mistakenly believes he is there to work on a new picture for her. On his way out he turns back and says to her, 'Aren't you Norma Desmond? You used to be in pictures. You used to be big.' She replies defiantly, 'I am big. It's the pictures that got small.' She then sings:

> With one look
> I can break your heart
> With one look
> I play every part
> I can make your sad heart sing
> With one look you'll know
> All you need to know
>
> With one look
> I'm the girl next door

THE SANEST GUY IN THE ROOM

Or the love that you've hungered for
When I speak it's with my soul
I can play any role
No words can tell
The stories my eyes tell
Watch me when I frown
You can't write that down
You know I'm right
It's there in black and white
When I look your way
You'll hear what I say
Yes. With one look
I put words to shame
Just one look
Sets the screen aflame
Silent music starts to play
One tear in my eye
Makes the whole world cry

With one look
They'll forgive the past
They'll rejoice: I've returned at last
To my people in the dark
Still out there in the dark

Silent music starts to play
With one look you'll know
All you need to know
With one look

I'll ignite a blaze
I'll return to my glory days
They'll say Norma's back at last
This time I'm staying
I'm staying for good
I'll be back
Where I was born to be
With one look
I'll be me.

Norma's other big song comes in the second act when she arrives at Paramount studios believing she is there to discuss her new picture with Cecil B. DeMille. The audience knows that the studio only wants to hire her Isotta-Fraschini car. She looks around the studio in a daze and is spotted and recognised by an elderly electrician from her old days. He calls to her, 'Miss Desmond! Hey, Miss Desmond. It's Hog-eye. Up here Miss Desmond.' She looks up and says 'Hello.' Hog-eye says, 'Let's get a look at you.' He then swivels one of the big lamps until it finds her. She stands for a moment, isolated, bathed in the light. Then, from all over the studio, murmuring among themselves, technicians, extras and stagehands begin to converge on her.

I don't know why I'm frightened
I know my way around here
The cardboard trees
The painted seas
The sound here
Yes, a world to rediscover

THE SANEST GUY IN THE ROOM

But I'm not in any hurry

And I need a moment

The whispered conversations

In overcrowded hallways

The atmosphere

As thrilling here as always

Feel the early-morning madness

Feel the magic in the making

Why, everything's as if we never said goodbye

I've spent so many mornings

Just trying to resist you

I'm trembling now

You can't know how

I've missed you

Missed the fairy-tale adventures

In this ever-spinning playground

We were young together

I'm coming out of make-up

The lights already burning

Not long until

The cameras will stop turning

And the early morning madness

And the magic in the making

Yes everything's as if we never said goodbye

I don't want to be alone

That's all in the past

SUNSET BOULEVARD

This world's waited long enough

I've come home at last

And this time will be bigger

And brighter than we knew it

So watch me fly

We all know I

Can do it

Could I stop my hand from shaking

Has there ever been a moment

With so much to live for?

The whispered conversations

In overcrowded hallways

So much to say

Not just today

But always

We'll have early-morning madness

We'll have magic in the making

Yes, everything's as if we never said goodbye

Yes, everything's as if we never said goodbye

We taught the world new ways to dream.

I first met Barbra Streisand about twenty years ago when she recorded a couple of songs from *Sunset Boulevard*. As most of you know the show is about a faded movie star who is desperate to make a comeback, or as Norma Desmond would say, 'a return'. Barbra wanted me to make a few lyric changes to the songs so they were more about a singer who'd been away for some time. I was invited to spend a day with her at her gorgeous Bel Air home. It was a magical day and I've since met her quite a few times at her concerts and I've also interviewed her for a Radio Two show a couple of years back. I will never forget sitting on her couch as she sang 'With One Look' in my ear with just a piano accompaniment. It was like listening to liquid diamond.

| MY MISTRESS

I always thought that if you were going to have an affair with a woman it should be someone called Kimberly or Ruby. I settled on Kimberly and I used to tease Shirley about this imaginary woman. We've always had a half-size snooker table at home and when I played badly with Grant or Clive they would shout out, 'Mum, he's seeing Kimberly again.' On a good day I think about moments like these and smile. On bad days I shake my head in disbelief that we can no longer share these private silly moments.

If I'm the sanest guy in the room then Shirley was certainly the sanest woman. She just seemed to have the right outlook on life. Whatever life threw at her she remained level-headed. She was always like this, she never got in a state about anything unless it concerned the family. As stupid as it sounds, although we spent so many years together, I never stopped being fascinated by her.

I got a card recently from Carolyn, an old friend of ours who had just heard the news. She wrote, 'Shirley was so kind and supportive to me when I had health issues and I will never forget that. A glorious, honest woman who helped me and many others so much. She had time for everyone. It was a joy and privilege to have known her.' After eighteen months it's amazing how many people still don't know. I was looking for a taxi a few weeks ago in Harley Street and I couldn't get one. I was getting late for lunch with Van Morrison and he's not happy when he's kept waiting. A car drew up and an attractive lady said, 'Hi Don.' I didn't recognise her until she said, 'It's Paola, Michael Winner's old girlfriend. Where are you going?' I said I'm going to Holland Park to meet Van Morrison for lunch and I'm going to be late. She said, 'Get in, I'll take you there.' I couldn't believe my luck and then she said to me, 'So how are you both?' I said, 'I'm sorry to tell you that I lost Shirley in March.' She cried all the way to Holland Park.

Shirley has missed so much this past couple of years. She would have been a great-grandmother twice! Ulysses is now eight years old and does funny impressions of Donald Trump. I have recently received a special Olivier award by the Society of London Theatres, and I am about to start work with Michael Flatley on his new production of *Lord Of The Dance*. Shirley was a huge fan of Michael's thrilling dancing. There was so much treasure left to share.

Life is very different now. I've had to learn to deal with direct debits, medical insurance, the AA, BT, Banham Security and a zillion other things.

I recently went to visit Shirley's grave in Edgwarebury Cemetery and before I got to it, I noticed another gravestone for a twelve-year-old boy. I felt this was a sign from Shirley to me saying, 'Look how lucky we were to have been so gloriously happy for sixty precious years. Now get on with your life and live! Live! Live!'

I still don't know where the stopcock is.

P.S.

During the Coronavirus pandemic I didn't leave my house for six weeks; it is a complete mystery as to how I got it. At first, I had a chest infection, then my son Clive noticed I had a fever. On 2 May 2020, Clive took me to the Chelsea and Westminster Hospital where they told me I had Covid-19.

I spent nine days in an isolation cell, where they pumped me with every antibiotic known to man and took enough blood to appease even Dracula's appetite. My boys were frantic. The odds of me getting out of there alive were slim.

I never legally changed my name, so I was registered as Donald Blackstone. No one knew who I was, and yet I was treated as if I was royalty. After about seven days one of the nurses googled me and discovered I was a well-known songwriter. When the time finally came for me to go home, a group of twenty nurses applauded me and sang 'Born Free'. It was probably the most emotional moment of my life. Many things have been said about the wonderful NHS but until you experience their love and dedication first-hand you can't begin to imagine how blessed we are.

I'm now back home writing songs and breathing. I owe it all to them.

Acknowledgements

My thanks to:

Grant, Clive, Nita, Cyril, Adele, Andreas Campomar, Jo Wickham, Gordon Wise, Adam Maskell, Mark Steyn, Laurie Barry, Donald Zec, James Inverne, Gay-Yee Westerhoff, Jayne Meegan and all the doctors and nurses at the Chelsea and Westminster Hospital.

enormousness? →